THE ELEMENTS OF

PENDULUM DOWSING

Tom Graves

ELEMENT BOOKS

First published in 1989 by
Element Books Limited
Longmead, Shaftesbury, Dorset

Designed by Jenny Liddle
Illustrations by Maja Evans
Cover illustration by Martin Rieser
Cover design by Max Fairbrother

Printed and bound in Great Britain by Billings,
Hylton Road, Worcester

British Library Cataloguing in Publication Data
Graves, Tom
The elements of pendulum dowsing.
1. Psychic phenomena. Divination. Use of pendulum
I. Title
133.3

ISBN 1 - 85230 - 066 - 3

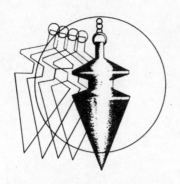

CONTENTS

1•INTRODUCTION

WHERE DO WE START?

A pendulum is a finding tool, a divining tool you hold in your hand. A ring on a string, swinging backwards and forwards like the pendulum on an old-fashioned clock. A fascinating tool. A *useful* tool.

At this point, right at the start of the book, probably your predominant question is something like 'Why bother?'. And the short answer, for here at least, is that it's such an interesting tool for so many different applications in so many different areas; a general-purpose finding tool. And it's all done with a piece of string, a weight of some kind, and a little thought (or, perhaps more accurately, a little sense). Nothing to it, really.

It's such a general-purpose tool, in fact, that many books on the subject seem to propose it as some kind of universal 'answer' to everything. It's the great secret of the ancients, perhaps; or the science of the future. Use a pendulum and you will receive enlightenment . . .

Oh well. If you must, go ahead; but you won't find much of that here. What you *will* find here is a discussion of toolkits, of markers and pointers, of positive and negative, of coincidence and imaginary worlds, of inventing realities, of parlour games and hunting drainpipes, all of which brings us back to toolkits, which is where we started. Because the whole point of dowsing (of which the use of the pendulum is a part) is that it is something to put to *use*: after all, things aren't exactly useful unless you *can* put them to use.

Putting it to use. That sounds like *doing* things: like technology, almost. Which is exactly what it is: a technology with a little magic. And in some ways a technology *of* magic, in every sense – a magical technology. The magic and the technology meet in you, work through you, are you.

So in a way it isn't quite so crazy to say 'Use a pendulum and you shall receive enlightenment.' Though perhaps that's too grand an expectation: a few light bulbs going 'click' in your mind might be more realistic. In learning the skills involved, and working your way through some of the mental acrobatics and other confusions that you'll find on your way, you'll also learn a few things about yourself. And that's probably as good a reason as any for learning to play with a pendulum: it has few equals as a mirror of yourself and your view of the world.

But none of this will make any sense unless we put it to *use*: until we move these discussions away from abstract theory and on to practical uses and applications.

That practice is what this book is all about. If that's what interests you, read on!

WHAT IS A PENDULUM?

You can use almost anything as a pendulum. All you need is a weight on a short length of string. Or perhaps on a spring. And that's all.

There are plenty of variations on the theme. Traditional dowsers might use a ring on a thread. Students at some dowsing classes I ran used anything from a plastic white elephant to a four-pound pottery gnome on a large piece of rope (which met up with a wall and became a four-ounce handle, but that's another story . . .). It's more common, though, to use a small balanced weight like a builder's plumb-bob.

It's a form of dowsing that you can easily learn on your own at home. And it's nothing like as difficult (or, for that matter, embarrassing) as learning how to search for water with a forked stick in the way that traditional dowsers do.

To use the pendulum, you swing that weight backwards and forwards; and, by interpreting its movements, decipher the answers to any kind of questions you care to put to it.

All of which sounds ridiculous: the movements of a plumb-bob answering questions? He'll be asking us to tell fortunes from tea-leaves next! Science of the future, indeed . . . unscientific rubbish!

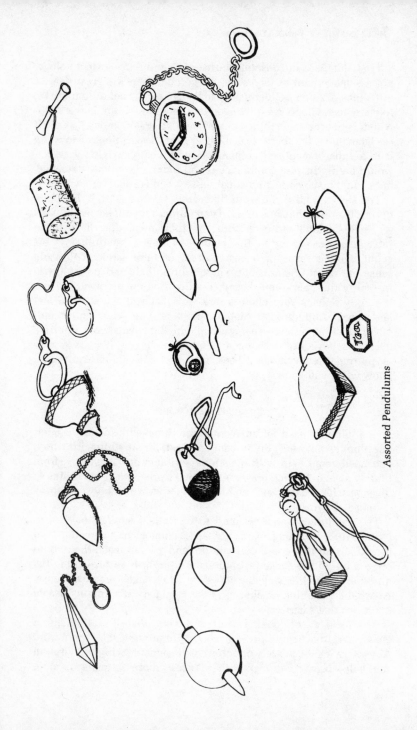

Assorted Pendulums

True. But then I did describe the use of a pendulum as a technology, not a science: and as far as I'm concerned, there's a great deal of difference. We don't actually need to know how the pendulum works: like any technology, we only need to know how it can be worked – which is not the same thing at all as 'how it works'. Indeed, as we'll see later, one of the shortest yet most accurate descriptions of dowsing is to say that it's entirely coincidence and mostly imaginary: which would hardly inspire confidence if you look at it only as a science, but should make perfect practical sense when we get there.

The key to it all is the word 'interpret'. Or understand; decipher; divine: all much the same thing, if you think about it. The pendulum's movements don't mean anything on their own, they have to be interpreted according to the context. Using a pendulum is all about making sense of a vast morass of information; collecting sense out of an often chaotic muddle of options and possibilities. In reality the pendulum doesn't do anything on its own: you do. It simply reflects your choices in a way that you can see and feel and sense. And through that, in practice, you learn judgement, discrimination, taste; more important, you know what your intuitive decisions have been. Using a pendulum, if you like, is a way of putting the technology back into that magic: of learning to know when you *know*.

WHAT'S IT USED FOR?

A pendulum is used for answering questions: and, for that matter, questioning answers. So it can be used for anything in which you need some help with questions and answers. Anything: from finding keys to finding errors in computer programs, from drains to diagnosis, for cooking and catching. Anything. Well, almost anything . . . it's up to you.

The pendulum's answers tend to be limited to 'Yes' or 'No' or (with a little encouragement) perhaps a number or a direction: but then that's all that computers can do, and we can teach them to do quite a lot within those restrictions. The trick is in presenting the question in such a way that 'Yes' or 'No' makes practical sense. As we'll see, getting an answer is the easy part: it's framing usable questions that's hard.

Another way of looking at it is to say that it's all inspired guesswork: the pendulum is a way of improving the inspiration! Anywhere where you rely on intuitive judgement, using a pendulum can help, because it makes the process more formalised, more reliable, more known. With practice, at least. Which is, after all, the whole point of this book.

How Does It Work?

Everyone asks how it works. The short answer is 'yes'. It does. Sometimes. Better, with practice. 'Next question'.

I'm well aware that I'm cheating here. But in fact people have been hunting for a very long time, in many serious scientific studies, for a sensible answer as to how dowsing works: and have been led round and round in some very interesting but definitely circular paths. We simply don't know, and all the indications are that we never will.

More important, we don't actually *need* to know how it 'really' works, because what we *do* have is a good understanding of how it can be used, how it can be worked: again, technology rather than science. During the course of this book we will of course look at theory from time to time: but only with the intention of using it to point out other ways of looking at practical work. In practice, that's all that matters.

If you really do want to know how it works, stop talking about it and just *do* it: then you'll know. Perhaps. But do it anyway: because if you don't, no amount of theorising will make it make sense. Practice may not always make perfect, but at least it makes more sense than theory!

2 • GETTING STARTED

CHOOSING A PENDULUM

Before you can use a pendulum, you first need to have one to hand – obviously.

In mechanical terms, the ideal pendulum should be a small symmetrical weight, preferably almost spherical but with a point at the base, and with a thread mounted through the centre of its top. It should balance well at the end of its thread; it should not wander around when you swing it back and forth.

Many 'alternative' or 'New Age' shops can sell you ready-made pendulums that match this ideal: beautiful crystals, finely engineered bronze or silver bobs, or purpose-built map-dowsing pendulums on a length of chain. And in addition to simple bobs there are oddities like the 'Pasquini Amplifying Pendulum' with its hollow handle and tiny weight on the end of a spring, looking like a miniature version of a fencer's foil; or the Cameron Aurameter, which is spring-loaded to swing from side to side rather than up and down; and many others, of course. And all of these come with price tags to match.

But you can just as easily make it yourself. It doesn't have to be ideal, and it doesn't need to be anything special: the one I used for my first experiments, as a teenager, was a wooden soldier from the toy-box with a match rammed into the top to hold a length of thread

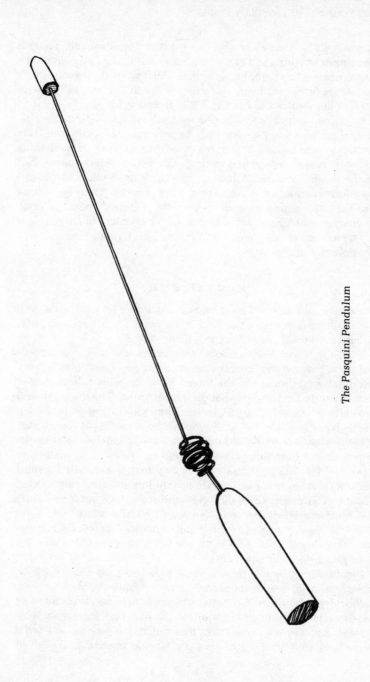

The Pasquini Pendulum

in place. Its balance was awful, but it worked well enough. You can use almost anything you can swing from your hand: I've even used a bunch of keys, or a bathplug on a chain. All it has to do is swing freely and easily from your hand. As long as it doesn't get tangled up with itself or blown about in the wind, it'll probably do.

In a way, though, perhaps it does need to be something special: special as far as you're concerned. As with any craftsman's toolkit, a pendulum can become something more than a mere tool: something highly personal, rather, that seems to take on its own character. Part of the magic, perhaps. A trinket, like the plastic white elephant I mentioned earlier; a pendant; a crucifix or an ankh; it may be nothing like the 'ideal pendulum' but it's something more than just a 'thing' to you, more almost a part of you. A minor overdose of magic might not be too bad an idea here: if something feels right to play with as a pendulum, it probably is.

HOLDING A PENDULUM

Once you have in hand your ring-on-a-string or its equivalent, you have to hold it in such a way that it can swing freely back and forth. Otherwise it won't, or rather can't, do anything.

Hold the thread between forefinger and thumb (either hand will do). Don't drape the thread over your finger: hold it with your hand pointing down, and the thread hanging straight down, rather as you would hold a somewhat distasteful worm. The thread should typically be about four to six inches from your fingertips to the top of the bob ('lose' the rest of the thread by wrapping it round your other fingers – don't let it dangle down to get tangled up with the pendulum). Again, this isn't a hard and fast rule – there aren't any hard and fast rules – but simply a way that works well for most people. Do it any other way and the pendulum will probably wander about as you use it, simply for mechanical reasons: but if you don't feel comfortable with the way I've suggested, that's fine too. In any case, you should certainly experiment with different ways of holding the thing as you play with it, to see what works best for you: it's your pendulum, not mine, after all.

Before we move on, there's small side-issue we could look at: the question of length. In some books on dowsing, such as Tom Lethbridge's delightful series, the length of the thread is meant to be used to select what you're looking for: the so-called 'long pendulum' system. If you've read about that, fine, but skip it for now, and we'll come back to it later. Right now it's simpler to stick to the 'short pendulum' approach. Where the length *does* matter to us here is in the balance of the pendulum – a heavier bob usually needs a longer thread of six inches or so, especially if it's used outdoors, whereas a lightweight one may need little more than an inch or two. It should feel comfortable and balanced as it swings in your hand; it should feel as if it's moving of its own accord without any help from you. But that's something you'll find out from experiment, from practice, from experience. Theory is there if you need it, but it takes a back seat to whatever feels right for you at the time.

USING A PENDULUM: THE BASICS

After all that, we now at last come to using the thing. Well, almost. There's one last point that we have to get clear. And that is that *the pendulum does exactly what you tell it to*. It moves because your hand moves. Your hand moves as a reflex response to something. It moves because you tell it to, consciously, unconsciously or otherwise. It does not do anything on its own: it's not apart from you, it's a part of you.

Like a computer program, it does exactly what you tell it to, and nothing else. In effect, you program its responses. You program your hand to set up those responses. Like the computer program, what those responses mean depends on the program, and on the context of the program. It can't actually go wrong, for the simple reason that there's nothing to it that can go wrong. What *can* go wrong is what you told it to do.

In theory at least, the computer programs I write can never go wrong, can never themselves make a mistake, because the machine can *only* do what I tell it to do. But I can very easily make mistakes in writing that program, so that I get responses that make no sense at all. 'This program's done exactly what I told it to do: so what on earth did I tell it to do?' The same is true of using a pendulum: 'This pendulum's given me exactly the response I asked for: so what on earth did I ask it?' As I said earlier, getting an answer is easy: it's framing questions that's hard.

What we're doing with a pendulum is using it to give a framework for reflex responses to questions, in much the same way as you train your feet to respond to danger in a car. Hitting the brake is – or should be – an entirely reflex response; but it's a *learned* reflex response. And one that works best when it finally becomes unconscious, automatic, rather than something we have to think about each time we drive a car. So the same is true of a pendulum: it's a learned reflex response, and one that works best when we forget that it's there. In other words, it's a skill, a skill we learn through practice, not through theory. Which brings us back to practice again.

KEEP TALKING

Despite my insistence that the pendulum does exactly what you tell it to, I'm now going to insist that it doesn't. In other words we tell ourselves that it works of its own accord, without our conscious involvement at all. That way we can use it to personify our unconscious response to questions: the problem with unconscious responses is that they are unconscious, so we need some way of bringing them out into the open, so to speak, to make them visible so that we can see what they are. And that's what we can use the pendulum for: to make the unconscious visible, or rather as a crutch to learn how to recognise the unconscious for what it is.

So a simple trick is to talk to the pendulum, as if it had a mind of its own, as if it were separate from us – which it does and is, and which it doesn't and isn't, at the same time. (I did warn you about some mental acrobatics! But don't worry, it doesn't have to make sense yet . . .)

Talk to your pendulum. Treat it as a household pet. It may have the personality of a slightly cantankerous child; you may need to cajole it, entreat it at times to give you the results you need. It may need a certain amount of house-training, to learn the rules of the house: that Yes means Yes, and No means No. And both of you will need to learn mutual respect. You can't force it to give you the results you want, but it will always give you the results you need: just remember that sometimes what you might really need is an embarrassing blunder or two. So just keep talking.

Talking to your pendulum is also talking to yourself. Yes, it's slightly crazy; but so what? I work in a computer environment where half the time people are cursing at their programs, trying to cajole them into working the way they want them to, muttering away to themselves and their screens: and that's just as usual and certainly no more crazy than talking to a pendulum. Much the same thing, actually. It's crazy, and perhaps a little inelegant, but it works; and that's really what matters.

KEEP IT MOVING

It's difficult to move if you can only stand still. In the same way, it's easier to watch the movements of a pendulum if it's already moving.

So, again, if you've read books on dowsing that say you should hold your pendulum still and wait for a response, fine; but note that for simple mechanical reasons (called inertia) you may wait so long that the response has given up and gone home by the time the pendulum actually gets a chance to move.

So swing the pendulum gently backwards and forwards, like a clock pendulum, ticking away the time. And perhaps watch it as you might watch a clock that's an hour or two away from lunch: out of the corner of your eye, with a little hopefulness, rather than full-blooded clock-watching.

Think of that gentle to-and-fro swing as a 'neutral' position. Nothing much happening. Nothing to report. Watch it like the hypnotist's watch – to and fro, to and fro. A neutral state.

From that state it can move to other states. The swing can move like a compass arm, pointing out a direction. And back again. Or it can change from a simple swing to a gyration, round and round; one way; back to neutral; the other way; back to neutral again.

Try it. Or rather watch it: don't try. Just do it. Let the pendulum move by itself, reflecting what you're thinking about. The pendulum, after all, does exactly what you tell it to do, since, as an extension of your arm, it's an extension of you: so swing it back and forth, and then let it go through those changes of movement, as if by itself. Knowing that it's part of you, that it's you doing it; and that it feels like it's moving of its own accord. That's when this little ring-on-a-string starts to become a pendulum, something you can use to look at yourself and elsewhere.

YES AND NO

The next stage is to set up a meaning for responses: at the moment, these wanderings of a pendulum are completely meaningless. All we have at the moment is something we call 'Neutral' and various other movements: so we need to set up some rules to say what they mean.

Note that *you* set up the rules. There are no other rules. Except that that also includes the rules which you set up but don't know about. Like telling yourself it can't mean anything anyway. And all the other hidden rules that you might use to convince yourself that you can't do anything new, or different, or unscientific, or in any way out of the ordinary. Actually, you can. Just add the hidden rules that tell you you can do it, rather than those rules that tell you you can't.

11

Be positive (and negative, for that matter). State what meaning those movements are going to have. Tell your pendulum (in other words yourself) what the rules should be.

Program the pendulum, just like programming a computer: give it a set of rules to follow.

Try the nice-guy method first. Hold the pendulum in whichever hand feels the most comfortable with it. Swing your pendulum gently to and fro. And ask it for a movement which means Yes. Politely.

Then ask it to go back to Neutral.

Now ask for a No. Any movement that will regularly mean No.

And ask it to go back to Neutral again.

(If you aren't doing this, you should be: otherwise none of this will ever make sense.)

Right. Try it again. Go through the whole cycle once more. Yes; Neutral; No; Neutral.

That's it. That's just about all there is to operating a pendulum.

Not exactly complicated, really.

All right, so it didn't make sense, it wasn't consistent. What did you expect – miracles? But if it really feels like the pendulum isn't going to play, make some rules: don't just ask it – tell it. For example, here's one instant set of rules: With the pendulum in your right hand, a change from a neutral to-and-fro to a clockwise gyration is Yes. A change from neutral to a counter-clockwise movement is No. That's the rules. (Or, if you prefer, any other rules you feel happier with: it's your choice, remember.)

If it insists on doing something else regularly, that's also the rules. In fact a better set of rules. Come to an agreement between you and the pendulum as to what the rules are. And make sure that both of you stick to them. You've got to live with each other, work with each other: find a way to make it easy for both of you, without you giving up and going away in disgust.

Yes, I know that this personifying of a lump of metal (or whatever) is crazy. I know that it's you on both sides of this discussion. It's just that this is an easy way for you to trick yourself into co-operating with yourself in ways that perhaps you haven't done before, to get at information that you almost certainly haven't been able to get at before, simply because you couldn't see it before. By playing this rather childish game, you can; later you can learn to do it without this charade and simply *know*. But that takes practice: something you haven't had yet. Just go along with this for a while. Play. Have fun. (End of pep-talk that was probably quite unnecessary because everything's working just fine for you anyway.)

With clear and recognisable responses for Neutral, Yes and No, you can ask the pendulum questions. (More accurately, ask yourself questions, but we've been through that a few times already.) And then get responses that you can actually interpret as meaning something. The catch is: what questions?

QUESTIONS. QUESTIONS

This type of dowsing is entirely about questions and answers: any questions. Any questions, as long as they can meaningfully be answered by Yes or No. Questions about anything. Which is why some writers on dowsing have presented it as some kind of universal panacea: 'The pendulum answers every question!' Well, yes: except that a lot of the questions you could ask, like 'Should I wake up this morning?', do seem a trifle stupid; and other questions aren't all that suitable in a system which can only answer Yes or No.

It's the same as people expecting a computer somehow to arrive miraculously at an answer to every question: even if it isn't designed for the purpose, or programmed that way. The acronym 'GIGO', or 'Garbage in, garbage out', is engraved very early on in every programmer's mind. A computer simply does what it is told, with the information it has available, and answers in the only ways it has available to it; and that's all. The same is true of using a pendulum: it's not exactly helpful if, in response to the question 'What do I do now?', the pendulum can only answer Yes or No.

So the trick is not so much the answers – they're easy, as we've seen – as in asking questions. The right questions. Except, by some Kafka-esque logic, you won't necessarily know what questions you've asked; and you won't know what the right question is until you've already found it. Fishing for facts. Hunting, pursuing, stalking a question. Letting each question and its answer lead on to the next question and its answer.

Almost all teaching in schools and colleges is still based on the idea of 'Here's a question – What's the answer?'; and usually with the implicit aside of 'We already know the answer, and that's the one you're supposed to guess to get good grades.' But what we've got here, as is true of every real skill, is something more like 'Here's this answer – so what on earth was the question?' Tricky, that. We'll keep on coming back to that as we go along.

13

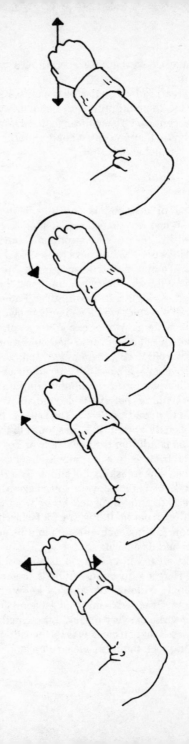

The Pendulum Can Only Answer Yes or No—Or Idiot

THE IMPORTANCE OF THE IDIOT

The big problem with a system that can only answer Yes or No is that it can't tell you when the question can't be answered by Yes or No. It can only answer Yes. Or No. Or perhaps say nothing at all, which is equally unhelpful – and leaves you feeling pretty foolish, and probably annoyed too.

All of which leaves you in the position where you can't see what's wrong. Like the infuriated schoolteacher after yet another interruption, you're saying 'Every time I open my mouth some fool speaks!' You can't see what's wrong, because there's no way in the system to see what's wrong. It wasn't built in.

This is where I have been known to get irritated at some other writers on dowsing, who present a rigid system which has only Yes, No and Neutral, with no space for anything else. And with no space, no alternative, no way to recognise that you've presented some dumb question, you'll be left stuck. Very stuck.

This 'space', which I call the 'Idiot' response because it occurs when I've been an idiot, is essential to any working system. The equivalent in computer programming is the routines and sub-programs that look out for errors while a program is running: perhaps the most difficult part to write of any program, because you've got to think of every possible error that might occur. And even then there's always something that slips through: there's a popular adage among programmers that says 'As soon as you think you've made your program idiot-proof, along comes a better idiot.'

Idiot. Un-ask the question, is what it means. This question can't be answered meaningfully by Yes or No: un-ask the question.

The way I use a pendulum, the movement that means 'Idiot' is a side-to-side swing, in other words at right-angles to Neutral. Check for yourself what that would be: try some stupid question like 'What do I do now?' and see what response you get. If you don't get a regular response, try the side-to-side one; change it later if it doesn't feel right. It's up to you, remember.

Neutral; Yes; No; Idiot. It wouldn't be complete, wouldn't be usable, without the idiot, the 'wise fool'. Which is you. And me. Of course.

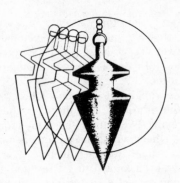

3 • PARLOUR GAMES

TEACHING AN OLD DOG NEW TRICKS

So here we are. There's your pendulum, hanging down from your finger and thumb. Swinging gently to and fro. And while you're reading this, it wanders occasionally off into the directions that we've determined are Yes and No. In answer to no particular question, but it does it anyway.

Exciting, isn't it?

Well, no. In fact you probably feel a little foolish. Twiddling your thumbs might be more productive. There's nothing to it – that's the problem.

Exactly: there's nothing to it. So little to it that you *can* do it.

Do what? Talk to yourself? A rather useless exercise. You're quite capable of doing that already, without having a pendulum to confuse the issue. You know by now that you can tell it to go round in one direction or another: but that's also a rather useless exercise.

The trick here, though, is to let go – to *not* move it yourself – or so it should seem. It moves by itself: except that you move it.

The pendulum moves by itself. Let it move by itself, as though it has a mind of its own. Let it be a servant, even though the servant is you being the servant of you.

It's easy enough to tell the pendulum to give you a Yes response when you know that the answer to the question is Yes. But that's pointless, useless. The pendulum only becomes useful when we put it to *use*: finding an answer to something we *don't* already know. Especially if it's something to which it would be difficult to find the answer in any conventional way.

But it's rather difficult to prove to yourself that it is – or isn't – 'working' if you can't find a matching answer by some conventional route. It may be fascinating to use your pendulum to establish the date of the decease of the Atlantean civilisation (or whatever takes your current interest), but unfortunately it's totally meaningless, since we have nothing else with which to compare that result. It remains entirely imaginary; it can't be matched with anything tangible. In a practical sense, it's useless.

Parlour games like 'hunt the thimble' are also useless, but they do at least match up with something tangible. The hidden thimble is either under the cup, or it isn't. (Unless you want to involve psychokinesis or something of that nature – but that's rather beyond the scope of *this* book . . .) Hunting for a thimble may be just as useless as hunting for Atlantis, but it does have a useful point: and that's to give you some practical experience – confidence-building experience, I hope.

What can completely blow your confidence is taking anything at this stage too seriously. What we're going to do here is play with a set of parlour games: with the emphasis on *play*. It doesn't matter whether you get it 'right' or 'wrong'; the only right or wrong is whether you practise or not. If you get it right – find the thing – it doesn't mean that you're an instant master dowser; if you don't find it, it doesn't mean that you're a permanent failure.

I'll say that again, because it's important. You're only playing: *the results do not matter*. The practice does. Getting your feet wet, so to speak.

I've never yet met a person who could not use a pendulum if they were physically capable of holding one. Anyone can. Whether they *may*, or *will*, is quite another matter. That's up to them. And you, now.

POSITIVE AND NEGATIVE

Playtime. Abandon seriousness all ye who enter here.

You can now get the pendulum to say Yes or No. Usually about nothing in particular, but you can get it to say Yes or No. These are polarities: opposites. You can use the pendulum to indicate a choice between any pair of opposites: Yes or No, positive

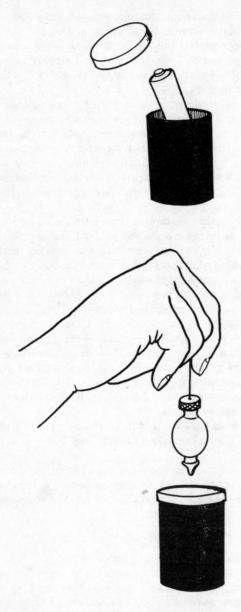

The Battery Game

or negative, masculine or feminine, yin or yang, black or white. With your choice as to which opposite will be the same as Yes on the pendulum: Yes could well be black, not white. It's your choice. Make sure the pendulum knows which is your choice (and that you know the pendulum's choice): talk to it, find out.

Let's play with a specific example. The two terminals on a battery are marked (+) and (−) positive and negative. That gives: us a polarity we can play with. So choose a flashlight battery, with a terminal at each end. Put it inside a small cardboard box, so you can't see which end is which. Now use the pendulum: is the top-side of the battery positive or negative?

Take some care over the question you address to the pendulum. It's pretty stupid, remember: it can only answer Yes or No. So you can't just ask 'Is the top-side of the battery positive or negative?' because it can't decide what you mean: it will either give you an 'Idiot' response, or else probably wander from side to side in aimless confusion. The question's ambiguous: in effect, there are several questions packed into it − 'Is the top positive?', 'Is the top negative?', or 'Is the side that is upwards positive?' (not necessarily the same as the 'top' side, since we tend to refer to batteries in a particular way) − and it can't work out which one to answer.

In the same way, watch out for, 'double-negative' questions: 'Is this the wrong way?' or, in this case 'Is this side negative?', because a No movement could mean either 'No means false' (it isn't negative) or 'No means true' (this is the response for negative). The Yes/No response here, in terms of true/false, is opposite to the Yes/No response for the polarity (negative/positive) you're looking at: a wonderful recipe for instant confusion! You do need to take care to frame each question so that you're always asking for a 'Yes means true'.

So ask a question such as 'Is the positive terminal on the end of the battery which is upwards in the box?'. Try other questions: note what differences you get, if any. Note down your responses.

Get a friend to turn the battery round − or not − in the box. Which end is on top now?

Can you feel anything else, along with the movements of the pendulum: a tingling, a taste, or something like that, that coincides with the way the pendulum moves?

Remember: it doesn't matter. Just play.

Do it again. And once more. Just play.

If it's inconsistent: so, it's inconsistent. How accurate were you with a tennis racket when you first started to play? Not very, surely. So why assume you have to be wonderfully, perfectly accurate with a pendulum now? Give it – and yourself – a chance. Just play. And through playing, learn; through playing, become used to the tool, become used to how it works, how you work with it, how it becomes an extension of you, just as a tennis racket becomes an extension of you. In time. With practice.

For a change, practise with your eyes closed: you can't see the pendulum, but you can feel it. Work on feelings, sensings, as well as on what your eyes tell you.

So practise that battery test a few more times.

Note the results. Just note them – don't concern yourself with whether they're 'right' or 'wrong'. It doesn't matter. Later, it will; now, it doesn't.

And with that done, let's move on to something else.

A pack of cards, for example.

You have a clear polarity, a clear pair of opposites in a pack of cards: the black cards and the reds. Choose one of those opposites to be Yes (in other words the pendulum will respond as if to Yes). Try it.

Make sure the pendulum shows No for the other. If it doesn't, make it do so. Practise with a few cards, face up. If the pendulum won't play, be firm – or something like that!

Now shuffle the pack, and turn it face down. Keeping the cards face down, sort them into what you think the colours are according to the pendulum's responses. Keep in mind what you choose as the 'right' response: Yes for black, for example, and No for red.

Keep your mind on the job. But at the same time don't try: just do it. Again, it doesn't matter what the results will be: you don't have to prove anything, you're not getting (or losing!) exam marks for this. It matters, of course; it also doesn't matter.

Go right through the pack. Face down. Don't peek. Don't worry about whether you're getting it right or not. Just do it. And remember to ask the 'Which card have we here?' question in a way that won't confuse the pendulum – something like 'Is this a "black" card?'

Now check what you've done.

If you've got the cards all neatly sorted into perfect piles of all-blacks and all-reds, then either you have an extraordinary talent (possible, but unlikely), or an extraordinary overdose of beginner's luck, or you've been cheating. The only person you'll be cheating, though, is yourself: the aim is to learn, there's nothing to win, it's only a practice piece. A useful practice piece, but certainly nothing to cheat over. In fact, it's much more likely that you'll have at least some mixture of red and black. And the piles are almost certainly not going to be the same size.

It's obvious that it isn't working perfectly. So you might feel a little dissatisfied – even to the extent of saying 'Why bother?'

Fine. We should expect that at this stage. Don't get down-hearted so quickly! You've only just started learning: you can't expect to be an instant expert after half an hour, surely? And remember, the first question in the book was 'Why bother?', and we went through all that then. So now let's look again at that pack.

Just how uneven were the two piles? Count them.

And just how well did you sort them? Count out each type.

Now realise that at this stage you'll be doing well just to get it only slightly better than random. One interesting point, though: did you get it more wrong than right – in other words did you put more blacks into the supposed red pile than reds? Because if you did, that's just as significant, statistically speaking: it just means that your pendulum is being a little on the unhelpful side and giving you Yes for No and No for Yes. Not exactly helpful, but it certainly means you're on the right track.

The key point here is that there's a knack to this, a kind of twist, a shift in emphasis or approach. As with any other skill, like riding a bicycle for example, it seems completely impossible to do it until you can do it. Then you have no trouble at all. But until then ... there's just something that isn't quite there, that hasn't quite clicked. Think back, or rather feel back, to that very first stage of riding a bicycle, when someone was holding you, and then you realised they weren't holding you any more – you were on your own. And you fell off, probably: at least I did (onto grass, fortunately). And did it again, and fell off again, and got back on the bicycle again, and fell off again, and got back on again, and didn't fall off. And didn't fall off much thereafter. Like you, I had learned the knack of staying on the thing. The same with that subtle balance of clutch and accelerator in learning to drive a car. And the same with a pendulum. It's a knack: tricky until you've got it, perhaps, but obvious once you have. Just like riding a bicycle.

Anyway, back to the pack of cards. Re-shuffle the pack, and go through it once more.

Check the results. They could well be worse. Yes. Don't be surprised if they're *worse*. That's usual. Two reasons: one, you're probably trying harder, and that's exactly what we're trying to get away from. The pendulum generally doesn't play if it's forced: you force away the knack of yourself working with yourself. And two, you're quite probably tired, and possibly bored.

Time for a break.

It's now tomorrow (it should be, anyway – if not, take that break!). Try sorting the pack of cards again. Check the results. See what difference there is this time.

If it's still exactly, evenly random, you could try another approach: just relax. Invite a few friends round, if that's your idea of relaxation. Have a drink. Watch a really low-grade movie on television. And try – or rather don't try – the sorting game once more; as a kind of collaborative game with your friends, if you did invite them round. Make sure you're playing: remember, you're not doing this to win something, you're doing it to learn: and in fact long experience suggests that you're more likely to make a mess of it if you *are* trying to win, to show off, rather than to learn.

Check the results. It could be surprising.

If it works really well, don't be too surprised. It *does* work, you know – if you let it. It's just that it's not that easy to let go enough to let the pendulum (which is you) work at doing things which our normal so-'reasonable' assumptions tell us we can't do. Actually, that 'reason' isn't all that reasonable in practice: so you *can* get the pendulum to work what may seem like wonders, once you manage somehow to forget those assumptions for a while.

As an aside, a gentle warning: don't go off and do this pack-sorting game ten thousand times now that you've done it well once. It'll bore you stiff, and what you'll see at the end of it all is an impressive proof of statistical definitions of chance. Once or twice we can quite happily ignore the rules that someone else says have to apply: do it many times, and the pendulum can't run away and have fun playing games with chance any more. We can argue indefinitely as to whether the 'rules of chance' really are rules at all, but in any case almost all our pendulum work will be done at the fragile edge at which those rules *can* certainly be bent, in some surprising – and useful – ways.

Anyway, enough of theory for now: let's move on to something else. Sex, perhaps.

Well, it's another polarity, another pair of opposites, isn't it? As with black and red for the cards, set up which one of the pair – male and female – will match Yes and No. Try it out over different people (followed by the inevitable laughter and embarrassment when you get it 'wrong'). If you want to be spared the embarrassment, try it over a group of puppies or some other animals that are available to play with. Don't be surprised if it isn't consistent: you may have to teach your pendulum about sex as well as about Yes and No.

Dowsing for the sex of an unborn child is one of the oldest traditional uses of a pendulum, too: someone would hold a ring on a string over the mother's belly, and interpret the movements of the pendulum accordingly. If you can find a friend who's pregnant, wave a pendulum over the child (and remember that you're trying to find the sex of the child, not the mother – you already know that one) and see what you get. Record it. You'll have to wait a while to find whether you got it right though.

There's a variant of this that's actually a commercial application of the pendulum, used on a daily basis in some places (in Japan, especially): sexing eggs in hatcheries. Sorting the valuable female chicks from the (relatively) valueless males pays off in hard cash. It also takes a lot of skill: but if they can do it, so can you. With practice. You probably don't have a conveyor-belt full of fertilised eggs to practise on right now, but you could well have a pond full of goldfish – in the park if not at home. Try it. Record the results, and check them any way you can. Try it on different animals, different birds. Interesting, anyway.

HUNT THE THIMBLE

After a little outdoor exercise, looking at the birds and the bees, it's time to return to the parlour for some traditional games like 'Hunt the Thimble'.

Guessing games. Inspired guesswork, with the pendulum to improve the inspiration.

Remember to treat the games as games. The results don't matter; the practice does.

So: 'Hunt the Thimble'. Three cups: the thimble's underneath one of them. You need to borrow someone else to shuffle the cups around for you, of course. But make sure they don't hide the thimble in their pocket . . . it doesn't help! Although you could check with the pendulum – a good example of where the Idiot response might occur perhaps? Hold the pendulum over each cup in turn: 'Is the thimble under this cup?' Play with it. Take turns with your friend, shuffling and searching in turn.

Computers again: if you have a computer available, it's quite easy to write a small program to simulate the cups and the thimble, choosing which 'cup' to place the 'thimble' under at random. Then you can be certain your friend hasn't hidden the thimble! Display the 'cups' on the screen, and point to each of them on the display in turn, looking for the 'thimble' and asking for a Yes or No.

Remember, play with it; don't go at it and at it and at it. If you do, you'll get tired; you'll get bored; and it'll stop working anyway, as we saw earlier. Just play with it. Serious play; but play none the less.

Now let's try a variation on the theme. Take three different teas, or blends of coffee, or three 'somethings' which look pretty much the same, and put them into three cups or jars. Hold a small sample of one of them in one hand, and the pendulum in the other. Hold the pendulum over each jar, keeping one corner of your mind on the pendulum, another on the contents of the jar, and yet another corner on the sample that you're holding in the other hand (a neat mental juggling act that you'll have had plenty of practice at by the time we've finished).

The idea is that the pendulum will react in 'sympathy' between the sample that you're holding and the contents of the right jar. Sympathetic magic – as old as the hills, or at least as old as people. See which jar the pendulum reacts over. Make sure it does react over one of them: don't let your pendulum play unhelpful games with you.

Try a similar trick with that pack of cards. The old game of 'Find the Lady': three cards, two of them number cards, one of them a queen; all face down. Which one's the Lady? How would you tackle that with a pendulum? You could ask the question 'Is this a queen card?' óver each of the three; you could try holding a queen card in the other hand as a 'sample' (or, as American dowsers would say, a 'witness') of the one you're trying to find. Or see what technique you could invent: because you make up the rules.

As a final parlour game, let's try 'Odd One Out'. Four objects – any objects – three of them with a common factor, the fourth the 'odd one out'. The easy part is to find which is the odd one of the four: just ask the pendulum, wave the pendulum over each in turn with the obvious question in mind of 'Is this the odd one out?' (Not 'Which one's the odd one out?' – that would confuse the pendulum, remember.) What's not so easy is finding out *why* it's the odd one out: in other words finding the common factor linking the other three. We've found that this one is different: so *why* is it different? If you ask the pendulum why it's different, it can only answer Yes. Or, more likely, Idiot. Not exactly helpful: we'll have to find the answer another way.

'Here's the answer: now what was the question?' *That* problem again. Well, frame the question to yourself, like a banner drawn across the windows of your mind; and, using a pendulum, or not using it, see what answers arise: check those answers with the pendulum. Instead of answering questions, you're questioning answers. From those answers, see what other questions arise: check the answers to those. And so on. Straightforward thinking, the crude sledgehammer of logic, is no help at all here: you'll have to be more subtle than that. Fishing for facts. Thinking backwards, thinking sideways, thinking any which way but in obvious straight lines – because that 'common factor' may not be obvious at all!

4 • THINKING ABOUT THINKING

THE IMPORTANCE OF NOT THINKING

Now that you have some practice behind you, a little theorising would probably not be amiss here, and might even make some degree of sense.

So it worked. Not spectacularly; but you did get some credible results. You've proved that, to yourself, in practice.

But *what* worked? Exactly. Whatever it was that worked, it worked best when you couldn't see how it was going to work. It worked best when you let it. And if you tried to force it to work, it didn't. The harder you look at it, the less there is to look at: it simply disappears into nothing. Yet if you pretend to turn away, and forget that it's there, so to speak, it comes out quite happily on its own and does what is asked of it. Shy little beast, the pendulum.

It's like looking at a dim star on a clear night. You can see it quite easily out of the corner of your eye: but look straight at it, and it vanishes. The centre of the eye's field of vision can see colour, which the outer field can't, but it isn't so sensitive to dim light. And the harder you look, the less you can see. Since our central vision is so acute, logically it *must*, it seems, be better for looking at anything: but it doesn't work that way. Instead, we have to flounder around at night trying to look at something by not looking at it, in order to get a better view of it. Strange.

The same's true of working with a pendulum: we can get it to work best by *not* looking at how it works. We can think most clearly about it by looking at how not to think about it. A maze of paradoxes: thinking by not thinking. Contortions of the mind – no wonder dowsing seems insane at times!

A CHAOS OF CAUSES

The worst mistake is trying to find out how the pendulum *really* works, where the answers *really* come from, what *really* makes the pendulum move. That'll drive you crazy. Don't bother, just get on with it.

All right: so you insist. You want an answer: none of my usual evasions. There must be a single cause, a simple causal explanation, surely? After all, everything else has one, doesn't it? Well, doesn't it?

Well, not exactly.

To be honest: no. It doesn't.

In fact *that's* the problem, that's the mistake I keep going on about.

We're taught in school that everything has a simple explanation, that everything can be shown to be caused by something else in a known way: and as long as you leave it at school-level platitudes which explain everything so neatly, you can indeed leave it at that. Everything fits, everything is certain, everything works within the 'laws of nature'. As long as you don't look too closely, that is: because it turns out that there are always exceptions to every rule. And those exceptions, we're told, make up a further set of rules, the ones we're taught as 'fact' at college rather than school. Except that there are exceptions to *those* rules; and so on and so on, *ad infinitum*. Those so-certain absolute rules turn out to be vague explanations that describe how things seem to work most of the time, probably, perhaps, as long as you don't mind a few inconsistencies here and there. You can just ignore those. They don't matter – honest.

And that's what we're told is 'scientific truth' (even if it doesn't bear much resemblance to real science as practised). Just sweep the inconsistencies under the carpet and they'll disappear. Honestly. A pity about all those lumps in the carpet, though . . .

You still want to try to understand it all scientifically? Because it *has* to make sense that way, otherwise it can't possibly work? All right, so let's try to be scientific, to break it down into a simple chain of events caused by other events, other causes.

First, we know that the pendulum moves because your hand moves. All perfectly normal, strictly according to the laws of physics: nothing paranormal about that.

Your hand moves because a reflex muscular response is triggered. All perfectly normal, according to the laws of physiology – or rather, as far as we understand what we sometimes hope are laws of physiology.

And the reflex response is triggered by . . . um . . . er . . . well, let's just forget that, shall we?

No? Well, you did ask for it:

It's caused by heat. Atmospheric changes. Ultrasonic scanning. Minute variations in magnetic fields. Radio waves. Geological and cosmic radiation. Interpretation of small clues in the landscape. An ultra-sensitive sense of smell. Special radiations that obviously must be physical even though no one's managed to isolate them yet. Resonance between the length of the pendulum thread and the natural vibrations of the object you're looking for. Telepathy from the cat, which somehow knew anyway. Accessing the Akashic record. Astral projection. A message from your deceased great-grandmother. A small demon reaching out and moving your hand. It seemed like a good idea to move my hand then, honest. And – the all-time favourite – 'It's only coincidence.'

A chaos of causes – or non-causes. Pick your own: there's plenty more in the bunch.

Explanations: they're all explanations. Any one of them would do: in my time I've seen 'proofs' that demonstrate that *all* of them are true, in their own terms at least. Any explanation you care to cook up. But in a sense *none* of them are true, since most of them are mutually exclusive and very few of them make practical sense.

And you thought there would be just one, nice, neat, simple explanation?

On their own, none of these explanations are much use, either. Each explains just one thing, and then limits the possibilities to look further: to stop you getting it done another way. The most common of these explanations, of course, is that anyway it can't work because it isn't scientific, it doesn't fit with the laws of chance, the laws of nature. Round the same loop we go, again and again. The only way out of the loop is to see that the explanation doesn't matter: the *use* of the explanation does.

Take an explanation which says that getting the pendulum to work is well-nigh impossible, and suddenly it's well-nigh impossible to get the pendulum to work. Invent an explanation that makes it easy, and suddenly it's easy (or easier, at any rate). Why make things difficult? Don't try to make it make sense in theory: it won't. Get it to make sense in practice: that's what matters. And you can use whatever explanation you like – however banal, however crazy – to make it work in practice: what matters is whether the explanation makes things easier, whether it makes sense in *use*.

That's why I keep going on about the pendulum being part of a technology, 'a practical art', rather than a science. Technology is *not* 'applied science': it may use some scientific ideas from time to time, but it doesn't have to be stuck with the rigid limitations of science at all.

In science, we have to pretend we know everything, understand everything; and everything has to fit within one interrelated structure of causes and effects, a closed net of logic with no loose ends. If something doesn't fit, we're in real trouble. That's why so many scientists get so upset about intimations of the paranormal: if something can't be forced to fit within the structure, it could actually destroy the whole beautiful edifice that's been built up over so many centuries. So the solution that many scientists go for when faced with oddities like dowsing is to say that because it doesn't fit, it can't exist. In reality, that's not science at all: that's a parody of science, even if it is a very common one.

But in technology, we don't have that problem: we don't have to make things fit. They only have to work – whether they fit someone's supposed rules or not. We quite happily admit the absence of omniscience, admit we don't actually know how things work, and just get on with it instead. We don't have a clue how even a simple thing like a light-bulb works in the way it does: if you take the explanations all the way down, you'll find that every one of them is based on unknowns – for example, we don't have a clue what magnetism or electricity *really* are at all. But we can use them. And we do use them. Using explanations that make it easier to use them, rather than ones that make it harder.

So let's do the same with the pendulum. We know the basics of how to make it easier: holding the pendulum so that it can move freely, or so that it doesn't argue with the wind. And we also know that thinking about causes, or trying to control the pendulum's movements rather than letting it work 'by itself', won't actually help either: we don't know *why* it doesn't help, but we do know that it doesn't help, and that's enough for now. Get on and use it. Don't worry about it. It's quite happy to work if you let it, as you'll find out in time and in practice.

GETTING THROUGH THE MAZE

Learning any new skill is a confusing maze. At first it works wonderfully: then it doesn't. At all. Beginner's luck lapses into neophyte's gloom, as you try harder and harder to get back to the ease with which you started as a beginner. Trying harder can be very trying: the bitter joke of 'Try hard to relax.'

I find it useful to play with that analogy of the learning process as a maze – or rather a labyrinth, the old single-path maze design that occurs in so many cultures. Single-path because you know you'll get there in the end if you don't give up!

As you enter the labyrinth you move almost immediately to very near the centre: beginner's luck, we call it. You know what the target is, but you don't know any 'right' way of doing it: and since you want to get there, you get there your own way, the way that suits you best.

Well, nearly there, at any rate. Not quite all the way there. Right, you say, how can I improve on this: and thinking hard, and asking around of various authorities who happen to be passing by (the opposite way, as you'll notice later), you try harder. Missing the centre. Skirting round it, in fact.

Eventually you come round to another corner. This isn't working well, you're getting no closer to the centre, in fact you're further away than you were at the best part of beginner's luck. Try another way.

And back round the circle: further out than before. Eventually you notice: that way wasn't right either, better try the way I started with. So back round the circle you go – further out than ever.

When you come back close to where you started again, realisation hits: you're further out than when you started! I'm useless! I'll never learn how to do it! I may as well give up now . . . It's what I call 'the dark night of the soul'.

But if you can make it round that curve, instead of jumping out of the maze in despair, almost immediately you're close to the centre again: a boost to your morale. Second wind, we call it.

But again things get worse. After skirting the centre again (from the opposite direction to your original path as a beginner), you find yourself working outward. The path twists and turns, until you probably feel you're going round the bend.

And then, without warning, you're there. At the centre, the place you've been trying to reach for so long. Mastery of the skill. You *know*: you have the knowledge of how to use it, of how to use you with it, through it. It's been a longer journey than it looked at first, perhaps. The only catch is: you now have to re-tread your steps to explain to others how you got there; and confuse them in the process, since you're always looking outward from knowledge while they're looking inward without it. Confusing; frustrating at times.

Every skill is like that. With most skills it's not so obvious – there's so much mechanical detail to learn for each, so many differing physical manipulations to master, that the sameness gets concealed. But learning to use a pendulum is exactly the same in that respect

The Labyrinth

31

as learning cookery or carpentry: it's just that there's so little to it that you can hardly see the learned nature of it all at times. But you can learn it; have already learned a lot of it, although you may not realise it as yet.

COINCIDENCE AND IMAGINARY

One ever-popular explanation used by people watching a pendulum going through its motions is 'It's all coincidence.' A generalised catch-all statement, that: anything you don't understand, anything which doesn't fit 'the rules', you can dismiss as 'a mere coincidence'. If you can't show the one true cause, in the best school-scientific manner – which, as we've seen, we can't – it can't possibly be anything other than coincidence.

The problem is: that's exactly what it is. The pendulum's responses are just that: coincidence. Worse, they're coincidences relating to things that are mostly imaginary. As I said before, one of the shortest and most accurate descriptions of dowsing is to say that it's entirely coincidence and mostly imaginary.

Which puts an end to everything we've done so far. If it's only coincidence, it must be meaningless.

That's it: it's only coincidence.

Except: we were actually getting some useful results back there. Your results may not have been brilliant, but you were able to sort those cards fairly well (at least, if you didn't try too hard); you were able to use the pendulum to find the right cup of tea; you could tell which way up a battery was.

To call something 'a mere coincidence' isn't actually an explanation at all: it's a dismissal, a non-explanation that's running away from explaining something because it knows perfectly well that it doesn't have an explanation. And explanations, as we've seen, are only useful if they can show us a better way to use the pendulum: if not, they're useless. Worse than useless, in fact, because they're a hindrance that can stop us from being able to do anything at all.

The pendulum works; or rather you work and it tells you that you're working by apparently working by itself. All coincidence, really. The pendulum's fine, and so is your use of it: it's the common understanding about what coincidence is – and isn't – that's wrong. And things imaginary, for that matter.

So we need a better look at this thing that's 'entirely coincidence and mostly imaginary'.

'IT'S ALL COINCIDENCE'

I have known people get rather upset at my description of the responses of the pendulum as 'only coincidence'. It sounds too dismissive: but, as you'll have realised by now, that isn't what I mean at all. Equally I don't like assigning too much meaning to coincidence: I've seen far too often the results of people taking every trivial event as immediate proof of the paranormal or else having some huge global significance. We can do without that problem, thank you!

My difficulty here is that I don't like inventing new words for the sake of it, and I can't find a better word than 'coincidence'. Sure, I could use Jung's term 'synchronicity', but I'd only be mangling that one too. Although a lot of people do use it in a sense of 'it wasn't coincidence, it was a synchronicity', in other words some kind of meaningful coincidence, Jung did originally intend the word to have a specific meaning in relation to *time*: taken back to its component root-words, it literally means 'the same time'. But the problem is that when we start to use a pendulum to investigate events within time – finding where something has been, or what the water-flow in a stream was like last year – the one thing we *haven't* got is 'the same time'. In fact what we have there is a coincidence of two times – the present and the past – in one place! So it's much easier to stick with the word 'coincidence', and use it in its literal sense of 'co-incidence' (with the hyphen emphasised) rather than the mangled, meaningless sense that most people seem to use so carelessly.

So let's get one thing clear. To try to dismiss something by saying that it's 'only a coincidence' doesn't explain anything: in fact it's an evasion, a non-explanation that doesn't tell us anything at all. A 'co-incidence' is when two things happen to co-incide, happen to meet in some sense: what we would call an 'event', in conventional scientific terms. And that's all it is: an event in which two things happen to co-incide, in space, in time or whatever. It doesn't mean anything by itself; but it doesn't mean nothing, either. A coincidence doesn't have a meaning: coincidence and meaning are entirely separate.

The coincidence, or event, has no meaning – it's just an event. What it means depends not on the event, but on the *context* of that event, what else is happening at the same place, the same time or whatever. In other words *we* assign meaning to coincidences according to what *we* see as significant, according to what we see as patterns of events. We see what we think is a regular pattern to a set of coincidences, and from that say that the later part of the pattern, the later set of events, is *caused* by the earlier stages of the pattern. That's an explanation: it fits the facts. But those facts are themselves all coincidences, events. And it's a moot point as to whether the pattern of events is really there, or whether we imagine the pattern to be there because it fits the explanation, and then say that the explanation fits the pattern because it fits the explanation because it fits the pattern . . . We determine what is 'real' and what is 'mere coincidence'; we *choose* what shall be considered to be 'signal' events and what shall be ignored as unimportant 'noise'.

We'd go insane if we didn't separate them, if we didn't filter out the signal from the background noise. We call it discrimination, judgement, but perhaps a better word might be 'sanity'. But it's our choice as to which is which. Our choice as to what is sane and normal, and what is not. In other words, we have another paradox, first described by Stan Gooch: 'Things have not only to be seen to be believed, but also have to be believed to be seen.'

This goes a great deal beyond playing games with a pendulum, so perhaps I'd better come back to the point: which is, how does this affect our use of the pendulum?

The answer is: a lot. Totally, in fact – because the pendulum's responses are entirely coincidental. What meaning we can glean from those responses comes from what we see as happening at the same time, at the same place.

But we choose to see what we expect to see, and have real difficulty in seeing what we don't expect to see.

We ask a question: and expect an answer. The pendulum's response *coincides* with the question: Yes or No. We hope. It gains its meaning from the coincidence of the question with the response.

The catch is: the *total* question. The *total* context in which the response occurred: not just the question you hope you had framed so clearly in your mind. Absolutely everything. And I mean *everything*: in principle, the fact that you had marmalade for breakfast last Tuesday and that it's raining in Guatemala at the moment could have a bearing on the pendulum's response.

In most technology we cheat, and say that only information within a certain set of limits will matter. We call those limitations 'the laws of nature'. And television pundits and others whose sanity and whose pay-cheques depend on you believing what they believe would certainly tell you that these laws of nature define the entirety of the universe. Which proves, they'll insist, that anything that doesn't fit these laws is 'supernatural' and therefore (by a rather neat piece of circular reasoning) doesn't exist.

In fact these 'laws' are nothing of the kind. The reality is that we don't know everything; indeed it's quite easy to prove that we never *will* know everything (other than in a fleeting, intuitive sense, perhaps). And if we don't know everything, we don't actually know *anything* absolutely. In practical experience and in the real world of trying to get things to work the way we want them to, the result is, as any engineer will tell you, that there's just *one* absolute law of the universe. It's usually called 'Murphy's Law'. And it's very simple: 'If something can go wrong, it probably will – and usually in the worst possible way.'

The trouble is, there's *always* something that can go wrong. Because there's always something we hadn't allowed for; there's always something we didn't know.

All the 'laws of nature' that we're taught at school and college and beyond are, in practice, only guidelines, a kind of default that we've found nature tends to follow when it's feeling co-operative. Murphy's Law, however, really is a law. An absolute, unbreakable rule. And that's final.

But Murphy's Law is only one side, the pessimistic side, of something that is more wide-ranging. Engineers are paid to be cautious, after all. So Murphy's Law has an opposite, a more optimistic side, one that is better known in the magical tradition and elsewhere: we could call it Nasruddin's Law, perhaps, after the eccentric hero of Idries Shah's well-known Sufi tales. And it's equally simple: 'If something can go right, it probably will – if you let it – and usually in the most unexpected way.'

The trouble with Nasruddin's Law is that it is completely anarchic and completely eclectic. Anything goes, anything and nothing is true, there is no definable cause or effect, just a sense that 'things happen because they happen to happen'. To get it to work for you, you have to allow absolutely everything in. Fishing for facts, if you like, before the ones you want swim away downstream and hide. *Somewhere* in an endless mass of information, all of it happening now and somewhen, somewhere: all of it coincidences, events. A meaningless morass – except that somehow you want to extract meaning from it, extract the facts you need to find.

In effect what we're saying in using a pendulum is that we don't care how the information arrives – from what source, physical or otherwise, or via what channel or mechanism, physical or otherwise. All we care about is that the *right* piece of information should arrive. And that it should show itself by provoking a specific reflex twitch in the arm that's holding the pendulum, so that it shows up as a pendulum response that we've previously defined as Yes or No or some other recognisable interpretation.

We don't care at all what the mechanism is: we invoke Nasruddin's Law, without trying, and see what we get. We get what we get – all coincidence, of course. But what it *means* depends on the context: it depends on us. The rules that define meaning are not defined in someone else's 'laws of nature', but are up to us.

This can be disturbing, even frightening at times: to get the pendulum to work well, you're scratching at the surface of a suddenly uncertain world, a world in which everything and nothing is true at the same time, a world in which things can be both real and imaginary at the same time.

So the world's uncertain: so what's new? The only thing that is certain is uncertainty; the only constant is change itself, and even that isn't constant. We use explanations to try to pin things down to a certainty, only to have them get up and play peek-a-boo with us just for the fun of it. The real and the imaginary become blurred, confused; yet it's *there*, where everything is coincidence and mostly imaginary, that we can do the most.

IMAGING – 'IMAGINARY WORLDS'

A classic mistake, encouraged by school-level ideas about reality, is to take the physical world that we can touch and smell and see to be the only way in which things can be real. It's such a pervasive part of our training in our culture's assumptions that it's not easy to see that it *is* only an assumption, rather than something which is absolute, fixed, real. For example, it's often a mistake to ask about something 'Is it real or imaginary?', because, once again, the answer's usually 'Yes'. Both, at the same time: not real *or* imaginary, but real *and* imaginary. Real – but in an imaginary sense.

Watch a dog or a cat sleeping. Suddenly, still fast asleep, its paws twitch, its claws come out, it makes little running movements. It's hunting, it's seen prey – in its dreams. Entirely imaginary – yet real at the same time, otherwise you wouldn't see the effects. It's not your dream, after all. But if the cat's sleeping in your lap, its claws will be all too real as they sink themselves into your leg!

Let's take another example. Imagine an orange. It's floating just above these pages. (All right, so oranges don't usually float in mid-air, but this one can: it's imaginary, it doesn't have to obey the law of gravity.) Look at it. Look at its colour, its texture. Look at the label they put on it in the imaginary shop you imagined you bought it from. Reach out and touch it; feel its texture, its weight, its scent. Give it a squeeze: feel it yield slightly. Now dig your fingernails in: mind that the juice doesn't hit you in the eye! And now you can smell it too. Strip the peel away. And break off a segment. Put the segment in your mouth: rest it on the tip of your tongue, like a small neatly-wrapped parcel, tasting of nothing much. Now bite on it . . . and as the juice bursts into your mouth, now you taste it! Except it's entirely imaginary. Yet you felt it, smelt it, tasted it; sensed it in a way that we could record and measure physically. So it's real: real *and* imaginary. At the same time.

Fine. So things can be real and imaginary. Very interesting. So what's the use, you ask.

The answer is that that's how we can set up the context so that the pendulum's responses can be meaningful. We build a complete image of what we're looking for; then, coincidentally, we find it. Entirely coincidence; mostly imaginary. That's how I described dowsing earlier: now it should be starting to make sense, even if it didn't before.

In a sense, we're playing with sympathetic magic again. We say the pendulum responds in 'sympathy' to the coincidence between what we're looking for and where we are. Without needing to worry about a connection or a cause. And both of those – what we're looking for and where we are – are defined, in part at least, in an imaginary way.

Normally we say we 'are' where we're standing, where we're sitting: in other words we define our position physically. But if someone interrupts me when I'm thinking, I might well say 'Sorry, I was miles away' – and in an imaginary sense that's entirely true. I may have been here physically, but my thoughts were miles away, I was imagining a place miles away.

Take a practical example. I'll assume that you're sitting down at the moment. Now, without getting up from your chair, imagine that you're walking out through the door. (It sometimes helps to close your eyes to do this, but then you couldn't be reading this at the same time . . . perhaps.) Look around you as you do so: what can you see? Looking through your mind's eye.

In imagination, walk on out into the street. Build an image of that street. Recall the image of it as you last saw it; then feel what it's like *now* rather than then. Watch the traffic go by. Hear the traffic go by, the chatter of people and birds, the world outside in the street; sense it, smell it, feel it. Go to the shop where you imagined you bought that imaginary orange; look around in there, sense around in there. You can, with practice, move about freely in this imaginary world, collecting information just as you would if you were physically there.

You're not, of course: it's all in your mind's eye, all imaginary, and real at the same time.

Imagination. Image-ination: building images. An imaginary world that's real enough to collect information from, information that could be of use.

Does anything stand out at the moment? Is there anything that's different, odd; something trying to say Hallo?

Fishing for facts; Watching, sensing; letting the world talk to us instead of us talking at the world.

It's that sensing that we're using in working with a pendulum. Building an imaginary world, letting the answers arise and show themselves, through the movements of the pendulum. In a sense what we're doing is using something close to a ritual to switch into a state in which we're looking in an imaginary world, fishing for facts, for information that could be of use. Using the pendulum to say 'look at this piece of information' – not so much an extra-sensory tool as an extra sensing tool that combines and links the senses together. Imaginary senses as well as 'real', physical ones.

The trick is to link the imaginary worlds to the physical one: literally real-ising the imaginary world, making it real. Without that coincidence of worlds, the coincidence of the pendulum's reaction is meaningless – 'a mere coincidence' – because there's nothing you can hang meaning on. The pendulum's response will be exactly correct, perhaps, but only in an imaginary world and not in this physical one in which everyone else exists as well. Merging imaginary worlds: another nice piece of mental acrobatics!

The other side of this is to prime yourself to recognise a specific coincidence – to tune yourself like a radio, so to speak. An everyday example might be when you buy a new car: you hadn't seen this model before, but now that you've bought it, suddenly they're everywhere. In fact they probably were there before, but you weren't primed to see them: so you didn't see them, or rather didn't perceive them. But now the coincidence has some meaning – 'it's the same car as mine!' – so it stands out as a 'signal' from the rest of the background noise of information. The result is that you can see it – although it looks like it's something new that's happening.

To illustrate this and to put the two sides together, let's play with a classic piece of modern practical magic: finding a free parking space on the street in the city. Sure, finding a needle in a haystack might be easier. The game depends entirely on how you approach it, and is a little like the old joke: 'You can have three wishes – anything you want – but if you should ever even think of the word "hippopotamus" everything you gain from them will disappear.' Now: you mustn't think 'hippopotamus'. What do you mean, you couldn't not think of it?

What we're trying to do here is imagine that someone will drive away from a parking meter just as we arrive. If you don't imagine it, it won't happen (or it may, but you probably won't see it, because you're not primed to expect to see it). If you try to imagine it, trying harder and harder, it will happen in an imaginary world, perhaps, but not in this world your car is in: knowing Murphy's Law, what you'll probably get instead of a parking space is a not-so-imaginary parking ticket. What you need to do is just imagine it; build an image of it happening; let it happen. And notice that it's happened – look, that man there's pulling out now. But perhaps it won't work if you think of the word 'hippopotamus . . .'.

If you don't imagine it, nothing happens; if you try too hard, nothing happens. Just somewhere in between is a tiny place in which Murphy's Law gives way to Nasruddin's Law; in which things happen, crazily, miraculously, irregularly, irreverently. Coincidences. They happen all the time. The trick is to notice them, to allow ourselves to see them as they happen. And to do that is like looking at that dim star at night: to see the parking space, the coincidence we're looking for, we have to flounder around trying to look for it by not looking at it, in order to get a better view of it. Strange.

It's not just strange: it's crazy, insane.

It just happens to be the way the world works.

So what kind of a joke is that?

MEET THE JOKER

School science has its law of gravity. Everything is grave, everything is serious, everything is known (by the schoolteachers and television pundits at least), everything is predictable, everything fits the rules. And you'd better fit the rules, too.

If that's your view of the world, meet the Joker. He's in charge of the law of levity: nothing is serious, perhaps, although everything is serious too, at the same time. And his rules say that nothing is absolutely known, nothing is absolutely predictable, and there are no absolute rules for things to fit – except for one absolute rule: which we see on one side as Murphy's Law, on another as Nasruddin's Law.

He has a very strange sense of humour: but then you'll have seen that if you've watched Murphy's Law in action. Quirky; anarchic; the whole point is that it *is* unpredictable.

In a way, though, it's all too easy to predict when the unpredictable will occur. It occurs almost without fail when you take things too seriously; when you're too certain that you're right. Especially if you're working outside of the so-safe confines of school-level reality.

That school-level reality defines little more than a cardboard world, a fake unreality which excludes vast areas of our experience, in the real world we *know*. But that greater reality is a crazy world, in which the key character plays practical jokes at whim. Not exactly helpful, but that's the way the world is. Especially if you're learning to use the pendulum to look at that world, to learn about that world. Because as soon as you think you're certain about anything, certain about how something *really* works, up comes the Joker: and suddenly, and often embarrassingly, things aren't so certain any more.

(I call it the Joker because that's what it feels like: perhaps it's more accurate, though, to say that it's us making fools of ourselves in trying to lay limitations on something that isn't anything like as limited as we are!)

The magical tradition is more used to such things than most. There's the Fool of the Tarot; the character 'Youthful Folly' of the *I Ching*; Jung's 'Trickster' archetype; to say nothing of the menagerie of 'non-human mischievous sprites', to quote a recent Church formal report on exorcism. 'The Devil, that prowde spirit, cannot bear to be mocked,' said Thomas More. In this sense the Devil is not a fanciful character with cloven hooves and horns, but an aspect of us: our own pride, our own certainty. If you haven't much of a sense of humour, cultivate one. Now. Urgently. You'll need it!

But you don't need to think too much about all this. In fact, in another of these bizarre jokes, it's best not to think about it at all. Just pretend that that school-level reality is all there is. Forget the rest. Know it's there, but forget it; let it brew away on its own. Thinking about it will drive you crazy: but then you must be crazy already to be using a pendulum at all, surely?

WHAT'S THE USE?

That's enough wandering in the background realms for a while. End of play-time; time to put it to use.

Except that it's never the end of play-time: unless you don't mind being the butt of one of the Joker's unfunny practical jokes.

Serious play then, because the pendulum's only useful if you can put it to use.

So let's move on to find some practical uses for the thing; move on to look at how to use it in practice.

Before we look at techniques and the like, we need to look a little more at what we mean by 'use'. Working with a pendulum, we are, if you like, working in a magical world, one in which matters of respect and balance are perhaps more immediately important than they are in the more conventional realms of greed and push-and-shove. Because there is this little problem which most people seem to prefer to shove to one side and forget: and that's the question of ethics.

Don't panic: I'm not going to wander off into some long moralistic tirade. It's more like the practical experience of an engineer. There are certain things you *don't* do if you want your railway bridge to stay up: you don't use low-grade materials, you don't allow shoddy workmanship, you don't skimp on safety checks and quality control. Reality doesn't allow you to cheat. Otherwise, all too soon, you've an expensive wreck on your hands, and some difficult explanations to make.

The same is true of the pendulum: you've got to get it right, but to get it right you have to be able to sneak into that gap between nothing and Murphy's Law. It's a delicate balance. One you won't be able to maintain, for example, if you're thinking about tomorrow night's party or what you're going to spend the profit on, rather than keeping your mind on the job. You have to beware – literally, 'be aware' – of what you're doing *now*, of the context of the questions you're asking and answering, all of the time that you're working. And, in principle, all the time you're not working, too.

There's another aspect to balance. Everything you do and everyone else does has its effects: whether you had marmalade for breakfast on Tuesday, and whether it's raining now in Guatemala, all have their impact in this crazy world in which everything is somehow interlinked without being linked at all. That means that you have to be cautious about what you do: you can't just barge in and grab. And that's practical experience, not spurious moralising. Look at some magicians of fiction: the sorcerer's apprentice in *Fantasia*, or Ursula le Guin's character Sparrowhawk in her *Earthsea Trilogy*. Then realise that they're not so fictional after all.

The Joker will be quite happy to oblige in assisting you in folly – with the joke on you. A little humility is a useful asset in using a pendulum. So is a little awareness of when you're about to put your foot in something that you'd rather you didn't!

So: how do you learn to be aware that you're not aware? More mental acrobatics?

There are ways – an infinite number. The right one for you is the one that works for you: only you will know which one it is. But one standard approach is to make things into a ritual, a fixed sequence – and then watch for 'holes' in the sequence. That's why so much pendulum work looks like inane ritual: because that's precisely what it is. Childish ritual; a game. A game with a purpose: putting a game to use.

The point about ritual is not so much in the content of the ritual as in its use as a tool to point out what's missing. There's nothing odd about this: rituals are used in every technology, although few people seem keen to admit that that's what they are. For example, it's twenty years since I flew light aircraft in the school cadets, but I still remember the standard formal phrases that we had to recite out loud as safety checks: 'Throttle closed, switches off' before priming the engine; 'All clear above and behind' before a glider launch; 'You have control' before handing over in a dual-control rig. Or keywords like 'hasel': meaningless in itself, but it's an acronym of a check-list – 'height, airspeed, straps, engine, lookout' – used as a safety mnemonic before starting an aerobatic sequence. Incantations in some high-tech mystical rite, with automatic, barely conscious responses. But we noticed straight away if anything was missing: that's what they were for. Built up from practical experience to emphasise practical experience, to prevent stupid – and dangerous – mistakes.

In the same vein it's useful to build a standard ritual to use with your pendulum to check that you're not about to make some stupid mistake. One of the most commonly used of such ritual check-lists is American dowser Sig Lonegren's: 'This is what I want to dowse. Can I? May I? Am I ready?' The dowser's equivalent of the pilot's pre-take-off check.

You could use it like a programmer's flow-chart:

Step one: Decide what you want to look for, and state to the pendulum, 'This is what I want to dowse.'

Step two: Holding the pendulum, ask 'Can I use the pendulum now?' (Context: do I have the skill to do this particular dowsing operation; am I in a fit condition now; am I capable now?)

If no (or indecisive), stop; otherwise proceed to step three.

Step three: Holding the pendulum, ask 'May I use the pendulum now?' (Context: are the conditions – unspecified – suitable to proceed; is it safe to proceed?)

If yes, proceed to step four; otherwise stop.

Step four: Holding the pendulum, ask 'Am I ready?' (Context: am I ready to proceed *now*?)

If no, stop; otherwise proceed to use the pendulum for whatever you want to go on to do.

End of sequence.

A checklist; a pre-take-off check.

Since we're about to move on to look at techniques, try it now: Can I? May I? Am I ready?

If any of the answers are No, it doesn't mean that you can't do it at all; it just means that you shouldn't do it now. If that's so, now's the time to take a break.

But you'll probably need that now in any case; and when you've rested, I'll see you in the next chapter!

5 · BUILDING THE

TOOLKIT

THE DOWSER'S TOOLKIT

Right: that should have been enough of a break. Time to get back to work.

So far we've only used the pendulum in a casual way: parlour games and all that stuff. We've also looked at some of my wanderings on ideas about the background behind these games; but if you've heeded my advice you'll have forgotten most of it already. You really don't need to think about it: just let it brew away quietly to itself in the background.

What we now need to do is to move on to look in more detail at techniques of using the pendulum: to look at practice in more detail.

One little piece of theory from the last chapter that's worth remembering is this idea that the pendulum's working is 'entirely coincidence and mostly imaginary'. What we're doing with the pendulum, then, is using it to mark the coincidence of what you're looking for and where you are: using it to give that coincidence some structure to hang on, to give it a meaning we can make use of. The information's always there: it's how to know when we've found the bit we want that's difficult. And that's where the pendulum comes in, along with the tools and techniques to use it with, to tell the pendulum (so to speak) where we are and what we're looking for.

Important point: *your* tools and techniques. There's no single right way to do it, no wrong way to do it – although there are plenty of inappropriate methods and uses, but that's another matter. There's no set method that always works the same way for everyone. It's up to *you*.

Sorry, but that's the way it is. It's called learning from reality, rather than learning from textbooks – which is a little odd, since this is supposed to be a textbook of sorts.

So my problem is to get you to find your own way to learn when you've found the right technique for you; and to get you to realise that what works for you may not work for anyone else, and may not even work well for you tomorrow.

Getting you to build your own toolkit, just as you would with any other skill. The cook's knives and pots and pans; the mechanic's measuring gauges and wrenches and screwdrivers; the dowser's toolbox of concepts and analogies and other imaginary tools. All much the same thing, really.

Dowsing, the use of a pendulum, isn't a 'thing', just as cooking isn't a 'thing'. It's a collection of tools and techniques which people use in any combination of ways to get the end-result they want. In effect, anything goes – except that you want a good result; a *useful* result. Just like cooking. Especially if you have to eat the results of the cooking.

A cook's tools are only one side of the story. The recipes are important too. A recipe is a summary of what you're trying to do in that piece of cookery, but it's useless without the practical knowledge that brings it into reality, and onto the table, ready to eat. A collection of recipes is a rather dull way of describing cookery: rather like trying to eat your words.

So with the pendulum, in which, confusingly, the tools and the recipes are combined in one, into the concepts and analogies we use as tools. A description of those techniques is useless by itself: it's *how* they're *used* that matters.

That's up to you. Anything goes; but it's up to you.

A LITTLE HISTORY

It seems that most people like to start with a little history. We started some time ago. Without looking at the history of dowsing and the pendulum. And we won't bother to look at it here: there are plenty of other books you can find it in. It's quite fascinating if you want to get buried in the past, but we're concerned here with what to do now. Not then: *now*.

The *use* of history, though – looking at the historical practices of dowsing – is what might be valuable here. For two reasons: first, there are a lot of interesting techniques that we can dig up, most of which were developed and improved and refined over decades of practical experience; and second, there are lots of older books on dowsing, both in print and out of it, whose authors insist that there *is* a 'one correct method' of using the pendulum and that their book describes it. Fine: that's their opinion, and they're entitled to it. But it *is* only opinion, not fact, and it may cause you some serious difficulties when you come to put it into practice, because it may not match up with the way you and your pendulum prefer to work at all. It may be true for them: but many of the old writers on the pendulum and related subjects seem not to have understood that what was true for them in their practice might not be true at all for others.

So I'd like to comment here on some other, mostly historical, writers on the pendulum, in case you've read their works and are trying to make sense of them by comparing them with what we've seen here so far.

There isn't much in writing about the pendulum before the end of the nineteenth century. Plenty on dowsing with the forked stick, the clock spring, the bucket handle and the German sausage, but not on the pendulum.

Then there's the French school of the 1920s and 30s, typified by Abbé Mermet and Henri de France (though both wrote somewhat later). They used 'samples' – a sample or 'witness' of the material they were looking for, such as we played with in the parlour games. They also used an enormously complex system of directions pointed out by a pendulum – the 'solar ray' and 'fundamental ray' – and of counting the number of times a pendulum went round one way, then another. The number of gyrations before the pendulum stopped was called the 'series', and the number of times the pendulum could be passed over an object and respond, before it was – so to speak – saturated, was called the 'serial number'. Just to confuse the issue, the series could vary in different stages of the serial-number cycle. These were all catalogued in the best scientific manner at the time: but the only trouble is that no one else gets exactly the same numbers, so the catalogues are not as helpful as they might at first appear.

At about the same time but from a different direction there's the development of 'radionic' instruments – the 'black box' which achieved a certain amount of notoriety in the 1950s and 60s. Probably the best-known books are by Wethered or, more recently, David Tansley. Radionic instruments are boxes with a group or groups of dials wired together in a specific pattern, which were set to a specific number: the 'rate' for an illness. The rate would be determined by changing the numbers on the dial, and you'd know that you'd set the right number by getting a 'sticking' response while stroking a stretched piece of rubber wired up to the instrument. (Later versions such as Tansley's designs use a pendulum held over a 'sample plate', in place of the 'stick pad'.) The rates for diseases were published in a rate-book, whose contents were taught as fact. (I do have a suspicion, though, that these rates worked for different people simply because they *were* taught as fact.) The system is still actively promoted by groups such as the Radionic Association in Britain; but it has no real applications outside of diagnosis and healing, which is not only limited but also illegal in some countries. It's also enormously complex, and I just can't see why it has to be that way.

Another common viewpoint of writers on dowsing in this period – such as Archdale in Britain or Cameron in the United States – was that only n per cent of the population (where n varies between less than 1 per cent and perhaps as much as 20 per cent) could possibly use the pendulum. If they had said *may* rather than *can*, I might agree with them; but I'd argue that almost anyone can learn to use the pendulum if they can be bothered to do so – and I've had plenty of students to check that contention against. This is important, though, because if you start off with the assumption that only a limited number of people can dowse, and you hit a few all-too-typical learner's difficulties, it's very easy to assume that you're one of the 100–n% of the population who supposedly *can't* use the pendulum, and give up when in fact you were learning quite well anyway. Don't be discouraged too quickly!

Next we come to Tom Lethbridge, whose books, mostly written in the 1960s, introduced many people (including me) to dowsing with the pendulum. I love his writing; but I can't use his system. It was based on the idea that the length of the pendulum string – the pendulum 'rate' – determined what you would find. Twenty-two inches was lead, silver, sodium or calcium; twenty-nine inches was gold, female, danger; thirty was water, west, green, sound, moon, age. Unlike radionics, a versatile system with concepts as well as tangible things; but every bit as complex, and dependent on Lethbridge's authority to convince you that the rates for each object or concept would be the same for you. It also suffers from a serious problem of practicality: with a string length of up to forty inches (or three times that long in some of his experiments – necessarily up a stair well!) the pendulum-bob takes an age to swing to and fro, making any experiments lengthy; and besides, the wretched thing has a habit of tying itself round your leg in the process!

At the other extreme, and certainly in more recent times, we have a stream of forgettable books, mostly from the 'New Age' end of the market, which throw any concept of consistency and structure out of the window. Instead the interest is more with what is currently fashionable than with practical utility: so we're informed that the pendulum works by resonance with pyramids or with the vibrations of the aura, and its sole function is to find the meaning of the Bermuda Triangle or to identify your true soul-partner, which it will do all on its own and without any involvement or responsibility from you. I suppose what really annoys me about these books is that not only are they mostly rubbish (though not always so), but they also tend to squeeze off the bookshelves some very good books (such as Sig Lonegren's *Spiritual Dowsing*) that have appeared in the last decade or so.

But my real prize on how to confuse people has to go to an Australian (whom I won't name) who wrote a book in the 1950s (which I also won't name) on what he insisted on calling 'radial detection'. Like the French writers, he built an immensely complex system of rates and numbers and directions. For him, dowsing was 'radial detection' because it had to be strictly by the sensation of any physical radiations, even if they couldn't be detected by any physical instrument. And in any case radial detection, he said, could only be done by people without 'imperfections' such as fillings in their teeth, scars or glasses. 'You've been to the dentist? Then I'm sorry sir, you can't possibly use the pendulum . . .' – which doesn't quite match up with our experience.

Some years later he discovered map dowsing and decided, by some extraordinary feat of tortured logic, that the respective physical radiations of the place were transmitted to the map and thence emanated for the 'radial detector' to find. More to the point, he said, only people without 'personal disadvantages' (no glasses, no scars, no fillings) could possibly do it; and even then it had to be done with the map aligned precisely north–south, beneath a bare electric light-bulb, at midnight. And not only had you to be standing barefoot on a slate slab (for insulation), but you mustn't have any clothes on!

Some method! Except as far as he was concerned, it wasn't *a* method, it was *the* method, the only way it could possibly be done. And if that had been the only book you'd read, no wonder it all seems pretty crazy . . . and you'd have some difficulties getting it to work too.

But the same is true of every book on the pendulum – including this one, I suppose. Brief moral to this story: don't believe everything you read in books! You have to decide for yourself what is going to be true – or at least useful – for you.

Which brings us back to another point of theory that we played with earlier. All these systems are, in their way, explanations of how the process works. Some of them a great deal more tangled than others! Each explanation describes what it thinks the process to be; you'll then see the process work – or fail to work – in conformity with the explanation. 'Things have not only to be seen to be believed, but also have to be believed to be seen.' If you choose an explanation that makes things difficult, you will succeed all too well in making things difficult for yourself. Choose something simple, something easy, and suddenly things can be a great deal easier.

What I'm trying to get at, I suppose, is that this vast variety of written thought about dowsing (including this book, of course) should be treated simply as a source of information. That's all it is: information. Some of it useful; some of it not; some of it a positive hindrance to practical working. All of it is fact, in that it worked in that way for the writer; none of it is fact, in that it may not work for anyone else the same way. It may be *useful* to believe, to *choose* to believe, that so-and-so's system is the 'right one', simply because it's easier to use a pre-packaged system rather than build your own from scratch – especially when you're starting. Just remember that it's your choice; remember also that package deals may have things you don't want in them as well as things that you do. Anything works if you let it, anything goes. It's up to you.

I do find it useful to treat any book on the pendulum as a kind of technical summary (which is, after all, what these books are), and to keep in mind a four-way check: is the method that the writer is describing *efficient, reliable, elegant, appropriate*? (This can also be applied to any other technology – particularly computer manuals, which are notorious for their unreadability . . .) The point is that many of these systems for using the pendulum are not particularly efficient, and are of doubtful reliability simply because of their complexity. They're also inelegant and clumsy, and quite possibly inappropriate for these times, or just inappropriate for you, now.

If it's not efficient for you, if it's not reliable for you, if it's not elegant (and elegance, a sense of *rightness*, does matter, does affect how you'll be able to approach your work), then it's not likely to be appropriate. And if it's not appropriate, perhaps you shouldn't be doing it – that way, at least.

Try another way. Invent another tool for the toolkit. And in the process, invent yourself; discover yourself.

THE DOWSER AS TOOLMAKER

We'd better keep moving. So, to summarise the previous discussion:

- No technique is perfect.
- No technique does everything.
- No technique works for everyone.
- No technique works all the time.

You need to be able to invent your own techniques, to invent your own ways of looking at the world – ones that match the ways that you work, in order to let you and the pendulum (which is also you) work together in a way that is efficient, reliable, elegant, appropriate. You need to know, that the *right* way may change at any moment. You need to know when to change method, how to change method, what method to change to in order to get the results you want, the results you need.

More mental acrobatics!

In a way we're back at that problem we've seen so many times already: 'Here's an answer: so what was the question?' A technique for using the pendulum is a way of asking questions with the pendulum, a way of framing questions so that the pendulum can meaningfully answer Yes or No or, in some of the techniques we'll see, a number or a direction. As you'll remember, it's easy enough to get an answer to a question, but knowing *which* question to ask isn't so easy. The same is true of deciding which technique to use.

The key is to learn to trust your judgement; to follow whims; to learn when things are going right 'all by themselves'. And, more important, to sense when it's time to pack and go home. Quick.

The pendulum is in many ways a crutch for your intuition, a tool to learn how to use your intuition and respect what your inner senses tell you as well as your outer physical senses, to use it to balance – but *not* replace! – your learned knowledge and intellectual judgements. Using a pendulum, with practice, you should be able more and more to note the sense of 'well, it seemed like a good idea at the time'; and to know, instinctively, when to follow up those feelings and when to ignore them. That's what we're here for – in this book at least.

The pendulum can be used to answer any question you put to it, and, to some extent, question the answers that you get back from it. You ask the question; the pendulum's response is not necessarily connected in any causal way, but is, strictly speaking, coincidence – which you can use.

What you're doing in using a pendulum is setting up conditions in such a way that those coincidences can have some meaning, can be of practical use.

What am I looking for?

Where am I looking?

What have I found?

The questions set up the coincidence, so to speak.

They 'prime' the coincidence; they set up the tuning of an imaginary radio to filter out signal information from background noise.

Let's look at this from another angle. What we're trying to do is to get the pendulum to respond meaningfully to the coincidence of what we're looking for and where we are. Each of these – what we're looking for and where we are – could be defined in any way at all. It's entirely coincidence and mostly imaginary: most of the tools and techniques are used to create images and concepts and analogies to define what we're looking for and where we are, rather than being restricted solely to the physical world. If you can imagine it, you can use your pendulum to look for it; if you can imagine being there, you can use your pendulum to look there. Entirely coincidence and mostly imaginary. Though whether it makes sense, to you or – perhaps more important – to anyone else, is quite another matter.

Accepting that you *can* play, usefully, in imaginary worlds can be quite a leap. That literal, physical, three-dimensions-only view of the world has been drummed into each of us for so long, from earliest childhood and right through our schooldays, that it's quite difficult to think outside of it. Our only regular contact outside of that is the grudging acceptance that time doesn't quite fit into that view in an easy way: time is something we certainly experience but can't exactly touch.

Yet we work with imaginary worlds the whole time. This book was imaginary, and as I write, of course, it still is: but I am making it real, literally 'real-ising' it, as I write, until it's this thing you're reading now. And there's no definable cause that you can pin down that dictates what I write, no single explanation that determines it, but more an indeterminate sequence of uncorrelatable coincidences that make up what we call 'experience'. And that experience is us. All coincidence, much of it imaginary. Living in imaginary worlds; making them real for others as well as ourselves, into our so-called 'objective' experience of the real world.

A shorter way of putting it:

If you're working with a pendulum –

- There's nothing to stop you working outside of the normal concept of space.
- There's nothing to stop you working outside of the normal concept of time.
- There's nothing to stop you working outside of the normal sense of dimensions and realities.

Having said that, it is usually more difficult, because to work outside of the normal definition of the world you have to get the world you imagine to match up with the physical, so-called 'real world'. And unless you manage to make those worlds meet within you – which takes practice and experience – it won't make any sense to you at all, still less make sense to anyone else.

Anyway, in the 'catalogue of tools and techniques' which follows, you'll find a free mixture of some techniques which are vaguely physical, such as 'samples', for which you might just about manage to invent a credible physical explanation; and others, like map dowsing, or using someone else as a 'pointer', for which, no matter how hard you try, you won't be able to make up an explanation that makes sense in terms of the school-level definition of reality. You could, if you really wanted to, use some wonderfully esoteric explanation about etheric fields and interconnectedness of souls: but it's much easier not to bother about causes and connections at all. It's pointless: the usefulness is in the use. I'll use any tool that's going, as long as I can find a way to use it that's efficient, reliable, elegant, appropriate. Anything goes: and I prefer to leave it at that.

There are two sides to this, of course: the tools, and the application of those tools. I've found it easiest to deal with techniques first, and as far as possible separately from applications. Although this may seem a rather abstract way of looking at the use of the pendulum, I've found in practice that mixing techniques with applications too early can make it more difficult to see how the various techniques go together and can be used in different combinations, to make up different methods. When we come to look at applications later, you'll be in a much better position to make up your own techniques: ones that work best for *you*.

What I have done here to avoid what could otherwise be somewhat of a tangle is to separate the techniques into three groups: tools for '*What am I looking for?*', tools for '*Where am I?*' and for '*Which have I found?*' (the last might be better expressed as 'What' rather than 'Which', but it's easier to see them as separate that way). The first two groups provide ways of defining questions for the pendulum; the last group gives you a set of tools for questioning the answers that you get!

TOOLS FOR 'WHAT AM I LOOKING FOR?'

We're asking the pendulum to mark the coincidence of what we're looking for and where we are. So, two points: define what we're looking for; and define where we are. Then we might be able to mark their coincidence.

First point: what are we looking for?

Remember: in principle at least, you can look for *anything*. But first you have to describe it, define it, which may not be so easy. Describe it in such a way that your pendulum (which is you) can recognise it when it sees it, in whatever way it manages to see it: that's up to it, not you – even if the pendulum is you.

So we have first to decide what we're looking for, and then to find ways to describe what we're looking for.

PHYSICAL DESCRIPTIONS

The simplest way to describe something – an ear-ring, for example – is to have it in your hand. Don't just talk about it, hold it. But since you're looking for this 'something' in the first place, it's not that likely you'll have it to hand: if you had, you'd have already found it!

All right you haven't got that thing. But you might have another one: the other half of a pair of ear-rings or cuff-links. An example; a sample; a 'witness'. Find me the same as this. Tell me when where I am coincides with something the same as this.

A lot of traditional dowsing works this way. To find something, you have to have a sample of it. To find copper, you hold a copper coin in the same hand as the pendulum. Or use a pendulum made of copper. Or drill a hole in the pendulum, and put the sample in that. (Many commercially-produced pendulums are hollow for that reason.)

To look for gold, hold a gold ring. To look for silver, hold a silver locket. To look for the queen-card in the 'Find the Lady' parlour game, hold another queen card. To look for a particular type of water or oil, put some in a small bottle and use that as the sample. To look for someone, hold a sample of their clothing: present the sample to the pendulum much as you would present the sample to a bloodhound, so that the pendulum can chase the scent for you.

Ask the pendulum to find the same thing.

Anything you can hold, you can use as a sample to search for something of the same type. In traditional parlance, this is 'sympathetic magic'.

Two points to watch for though:

First, it has to be something you can *hold*. It has to be tangible. For example, you can't hold a sample of profit, or of 'my soul-partner': they're ideas or concepts, not things you can touch or carry around with you.

Second, the *context* is important. Using one ear-ring as a sample, make it clear to your pendulum (in other words yourself, remember), that you're using it as a sample to find the missing ear-ring. Not the one you're using as a sample – you've already found that. Using a copper coin to look for coins in general, make it clear that you're looking for coins, and not just any old variant of copper such as someone's discarded plumbing or the copper knob off an old brass kettle.

Each sample has many properties: a coin is a particular size, a particular weight, a particular shape, a specific material. With the context that *you* choose, you select which property or properties you're using the sample for. By saying 'I'm using this coin to look for coins' you are, in effect, saying that you're keeping only the 'coin' property and looking for coins of any material – from gold to plastic toy money – and discarding the other properties such as size and weight and content. So you could use a copper coin to look for gold coins, if that's what interested you. As long as you made the context clear to yourself and to the pendulum. The question gains its meaning from the context.

The advantage of this way of working, with something you can feel and touch and hold, is that you don't have to think about it. Not that you should think about it, of course. But more that it has a sense of immediacy – *this* is what I'm looking for – and a sense of direct contact that isn't so easy to get with the more abstract approaches to defining what you're looking for, that we'll be seeing shortly.

In traditional dowsing techniques a 'sample' can be used for more than a strict physical correspondence. We came across an example earlier, in the parlour games: we used a gold ring – gold as an *analogy* for female – in trying to find the sex of an unborn child. If the pendulum went clockwise, a 'Yes' response, it's female; if counter-clockwise, a 'No' response, it's not in sympathy with the analogy, so it's not female – and so, presumably, male.

This use of an analogy as a tool is what is sometimes called 'sympathetic magic': the analogies can be used in a symbolic way – 'gold for female' – or a literal way – 'gold for gold'. Some of the standard techniques used in medical dowsing look as though they come straight out of traditional witchcraft: using a bloodspot on a piece of paper, a lock of hair or a small bottle containing nail-clippings as a sample of the patient being treated. In radiesthetic practice ('radiesthesia' being one of the names given by dowsers to the specifically medical applications of dowsing with the pendulum), doing various things to this sample, such as leaving it with a sample of some homoeopathic remedy, is held to have the same effect as giving the homoeopathic remedy directly to the patient.

It's what would traditionally be called 'action at a distance'. Under certain conditions, depending on the people concerned as much as on the technique, it works at least as well as conventional scientific medicine. It's also, strictly speaking, coincidence. The requisite result occurred, the patient got better; but quite how, we don't really know. We know that it works, but we can't tell *how* it works – we certainly can't pin down 'one true cause' in the best school-scientific sense. What it does suggest though is that perhaps we ought to treat the views of so-called primitive peoples about the magical use of images such as photographs with a little more respect.

IMAGES AS DESCRIPTIONS

Having a physical sample of something at hand is fine if you can actually hold it. It's not so practical, though, if you can't hold that 'something', such as radio waves; and in many cases it's inadvisable, such as when you're looking for diseases during a diagnosis.

So you can cheat: you don't have to have it in your hand. You can *imagine* it, visualise it, just as we did with that imaginary orange earlier.

Use an image as a 'sample': entirely coincidence, mostly imaginary; put to use.

There are any number of ways to imagine something. I certainly couldn't describe them all. But let's take some obvious ones.

You could write down what you're looking for, and use that as a sample. Instead of holding a coin and saying 'I'm looking for coins like this one', you can write on a piece of paper 'I'm looking for coins', and hold the piece of paper instead of the coin. Again, you'd tell yourself and the pendulum 'I'm looking for coins': you're using the piece of paper as an *aide-memoire*, if you like.

You could simply say what you're looking for. Just tell yourself and the pendulum 'I'm looking for coins,' without bothering with the piece of paper. You could recite the statement about what you're looking for, as if it were some kind of magic spell, perhaps. Say it out loud if it helps, as a kind of ritual: a formal statement, like the ones I used when learning to fly aircraft. You could almost repeat it as a kind of chant, a *mantram* – though perhaps it's not wise to do that in public! There's nothing to stop you saying it silently – which is effectively the same as writing it down.

You can use a picture, a photograph, a drawing, in place of the coin, and hold that instead: 'This picture represents the coins that I'm looking for.' It usually helps – makes things easier, and perhaps more reliable – if the picture is accurate: it's a better *aide-memoire* if it is. But since you're using it not as a specific sample but as something to help you imagine something else, a rough sketch might do just as well – it's up to you.

You can use something else, something completely different, as an analogy for what you're looking for. An example of this is the Mager Disc, a tool used by many water-dowsers to assess the quality of the water that they've found. This is just a plastic disc with eight segments of different colours. We say that each colour *corresponds* to a particular quality of water: yellow for sulphur, red for iron, grey for usable but low-quality, white for pure, and black for water to avoid at all costs. Or, according to others, black is beautiful: it depends on *your* choice of analogy. To use the tool, hold the disc by one segment, one colour, and ask the pendulum if the quality of the water matches that particular colour; if it corresponds to, resonates with, or whatever, that colour. Go all the way round the disc, recording whether the pendulum answers Yes or No (or, for that matter, Idiot) for each colour.

You could use a number to represent what you're looking for: you could call this the 'restaurant menu' technique. 'Can I have a number 46, please?' The extreme example of this approach is the radionic box, in which every possible combination of diseases is allowed for as a 'rate'-setting on the dials of the instrument. When the right number is set up on the dials, the pendulum or the stick-pad gives a Yes response. But any problem which can be reduced to a standardised set of answers in a numbered list could be handled in this way.

Or you could use a pattern or a picture as an analogy to represent something. In this sense there's a lot of similarity between using a pendulum and using one of the classic divinatory tools such as the Tarot or the *I Ching*. The main difference is that with the pendulum we're specifically asking a single question and aiming for a single answer, whereas with the Tarot we're using the rich symbolism of the card designs, developed over centuries, as allegories rather than analogies, to look at a general background in an overall way. Again, like the pendulum,'entirely coincidence and mostly imaginary': like the pendulum, just another collection of tools – psychological tools, I suppose – to be *used* rather than worried about.

The simplest method of all though is just to ask a question, expecting Yes or No. Of course it has to be a question that can usefully be answered by Yes or No – or Idiot.

So here we need to look back at what we did in those parlour games we played earlier, where we had a go at working with a question-and-answer routine. You'll know by now that the most difficult part is finding the right question to ask. Just like the scientist whose experiment has to test just one variable in the overall hypothesis, we have to find a way of phrasing a question in such a way that it can be answered unambiguously by Yes or No, or by any one of a variety of polarities such as positive/negative, masculine/feminine, high/low, or whatever.

The difficult part is making the question unambiguous. If you remember, we saw in trying to find which way up the battery was that we couldn't just ask 'which way up is the battery?', because the pendulum would just answer Yes. Even the question 'Is the top-side positive' wasn't as unambiguous as it sounded, because we tend to think of the knob on the positive end of the battery as the top anyway, so the answer could be Yes regardless of which way up the battery was. Not exactly helpful.

There are two booby-traps that you need to watch out for: double-questions such as 'Is this positive or negative?'; and double-negatives such as 'Is this not the right way to go?', in which a No response could mean either No – it's not the wrong way, so it's the right way – or Negative – it's the negative or wrong way.

A little story by way of illustration. Before the battle of Salamis, near Athens in Greece, the Persian king Xerxes asked his soothsayers what the outcome of the battle would be. They told him that a great army would be destroyed. He was very pleased with that: he had his throne set up on the cliffs above Salamis to watch the fray, confident of victory. But what Xerxes *hadn't* remembered to ask the soothsayers was *which* army would be destroyed: and unfortunately for him, it was his own.

By the time you've worked out a way of phrasing that really is unambiguous, you tend to end up with questions that sound like pieces of legal jargon: 'Is it the positive terminal on the end of the battery which is upwards in the box?' You can't assume anything, because those assumptions – including the ones you've forgotten about, and the assumptions you aren't even conscious of precisely because they're unconscious – all become part of the question you're addressing to the pendulum. Any question you address to the pendulum, you're really addressing to yourself, the unconscious side of yourself: and the unconscious tends to take things very literally.

It's useful to treat the pendulum as if it's dumb and stupid, as if it answers all questions literally, because that way you can begin to learn just what assumptions and prejudices you're approaching things with. It's not so easy to do that with the more allegorical tools like the Tarot: it's all too easy to wallow in symbolism rather than getting on with the job. But ask a simple question, and you'll get a simple answer. We hope.

If nothing else, it's good exercise in thinking!

This question-and-answer system is probably the key to using a pendulum. Once you've grasped how to frame questions clearly, you'll find that the answers arise by themselves – sometimes, and increasingly, without the pendulum, as though the pendulum isn't necessary in the process. Which it isn't – it's been you doing it all along. But it's a good tool to help you learn how to use yourself (that wider, more aware aspect of yourself) in ways you hadn't tried before.

Question-and-answer is also the easiest way of dealing with quantity questions: 'How much?', 'How many?'. If you followed the advice of writers like Lethbridge, you simply count how many – literally, count one turn as one whatever-it-is that you're counting. Which can be *slow*. Tedious. If not to say boring. Boring enough to send you to sleep, if you're counting a few thousand turns, as Lethbridge did with some of his dating experiments. Instead, it's much simpler to ask 'Is it more than . . .?', 'Is it (this much)?', and so on. A stream of questions with Yes/No answers, carefully chosen, can lead you to an exact quantity – with practice of course.

We'll come back to refinements on this, and many other aspects of the question-and-answer system of using the pendulum, when we look at 'tools for which' shortly, tools for finding out what it is that we've found. For now, though, let's look at some ways of describing where you are, from the pendulum's point of view, so that we can complete this whole business of using the pendulum to mark the coincidence of what you're looking for and where you are.

TOOLS FOR 'WHERE AM I?'

If you don't know how to mark where you are, the pendulum won't know when what you're looking for coincides with where you are. Obvious, really. So you have to have some way of telling the pendulum where you are – and that's not so obvious.

Even if we were playing by strictly physical rules we'd have a little difficulty here. The obvious place that's 'where we are' is directly underneath the pendulum. Except that it's moving. So where is the place exactly?

We can't get away with assuming that 'here' is just 'somewhere round here, roughly beneath the pendulum', because you'll soon discover that we often have to be accurate down to fractions of an inch, or work at the same time on places that are miles apart.

So we can't just assume: we have to *define* our position as we work – which is what the following tools are all about.

MARKING THE PLACE

The problem is that 'I am where I am' is ambiguous. And we know the pendulum has problems with things that are ambiguous. You could say that 'I am' where my feet are. And my feet are on the floor, sure; but where is the pendulum? It's not attached to the tips of my toes, after all – or at least that's not an easy way to hold it, and even then the whole point is that it would be moving around. There's no single place that we can assume is 'here' as far as the pendulum is concerned. Just to complicate matters, or rather to make things more versatile, we're not just limited to places or workings physical: as we saw earlier, the question 'Is it real or imaginary?' is a little too restricting to deal with the real world we experience.

You have to be explicit: you can't assume that 'here' is obvious to your none-too-bright pendulum. It's too confusing for the poor little brute: it's rather like saying 'I am where I am' and then realising 'Yes – but which I is me?'

So tell it. Define it.

If you're walking, the easiest way to define 'here' is to say that it's the leading edge of the leading foot. As you move forward, 'here' moves forward with you, moving smoothly forward as each foot moves in front of the other while you walk. When you get a response from the pendulum, stop and move back; the pendulum should go back to Neutral. Move one foot slowly over where you walked a moment ago: as your toes pass over the place where the response occurred before, the pendulum should react exactly as your foot marks the spot. Bring the foot back, and the pendulum should revert to Neutral again; forward again, and it should respond once more. Marking here; marking the coincidence between what you're looking for and where you are.

Another booby-trap though: watch out for the assumption 'I got a response here before so I ought to get one here now.' The fact is you may have been wrong the first time. Each time you look, try to approach it as if you've never been there before: an exercise in instant amnesia perhaps?

If you're trying to find a place that's not on the floor, such as in a cupboard or within a wall, you can't really walk over such places. (I have seen people try to do just that, but it's not exactly practical!) But remember, you make up the rules: there's no reason why you can't change them to something more sensible. So, to use the telephone company's phrase, 'let your fingers do the walking': tell yourself and the pendulum that 'here' is marked by the tip of your finger. Walking up the wall: 'I am where I touch.' This also gives you more precision than trying to balance on one foot, moving one leg backwards and forwards: instead, you can simply move your finger over the space.

It's not that using your fingers as markers is better than using your feet: it's simply that it's more useful in certain circumstances. If you asked me which technique was best, you'd get my infamous answer of Yes. Because both techniques are best: but 'best' depends on what you're trying to do. Choose whichever method is more appropriate now, rather than slavishly following what some book says. You choose. If you have to cover a lot of ground with the pendulum, you're better off walking, using that 'leading edge of the leading foot' as a marker: you don't have to crawl around a field on your hands and knees!

POINTING THE WAY

Walking around sounds too much like hard work. Exercise, even! I'd rather take it easy . . .

If you want to stay lazy, you can. It may not be as reliable, but in principle you can do everything from your armchair. (Well, almost everything . . .) All you have to do is point the way.

If you think about it, that's what you've been doing already. You're pointing to a place with 'the leading edge of the leading foot'; you're pointing to a place with your fingertips. You're touching the surface, perhaps, so to an extent you're dealing with something tangible there, you're marking your position in a physical way. Except that you're *choosing* which part of your body is *the* marker. It's not something that's fixed: it's your choice. You could just as easily declare that 'here' is marked by the tip of your nose – just as easy but not as practical, though.

So you can choose other ways to mark 'here'. For example, let's say that you're walking through a field, following the line of a pipe. It's headed towards a corner of the next field. Up to this point you've been using your feet to mark 'here' as you walk; but to follow the line further you've not only to cross into the next farmer's land (and he's not going to be happy about that), but also to wade through a nice muddy ditch and scramble under a bramble hedge. Not a pleasant prospect. Yet you've already found that the pipe comes out into this farmer's next field, off to the right – it only goes through a corner of the other farmer's field.

Too much like hard work. It may be more reliable to get your clothes shredded by the hedge, but it's hardly elegant! So you can cheat. Let your eyes do the walking, so to speak, and define that 'here' is where you're looking at. Try to see the pipe underground, with imaginary eyes; let the pendulum tell you when you're on track, or when you're moving off it. You can get it to tell you which direction to go – even though you're not going to go there yourself.

To get the pendulum to give you directions, we change its rules a little. So far we've said that we only have four states for the pendulum to be in: Yes, No, Neutral and Idiot. But you'll have noticed by now that there are any number of intermediate states, as it moves from one main mode to another. There's a state that's a 'sort-of-Yes', where it does a half-hearted attempt at gyration. There's a 'sort-of-Idiot', where it swings backwards and forwards along a line that's neither Neutral nor Idiot, but somewhere in between. To some extent this is the pendulum answering questions that you don't know you've asked: the pendulum's way of dealing with ambiguity, perhaps. But just as we've invented, or set up, a number of responses whose meanings we know, so we can add others to the list, and derive meaning from them too.

What we're now going to say is that we want a direction, so would the pendulum please be polite enough to show it to us? In other words, starting from Neutral, we want it to continue to swing back and forth, but that the *line* of the swing should move to point out a direction. Rather like 'the leading edge of the leading foot', the leading edge of the swing points out the direction – the front of the swing, not the back.

You could try that now as an exercise. Swing the pendulum in the Neutral state. Ask the pendulum to point to the north (True or Magnetic – take your choice). The direction of the neutral swing should move in such a way that the front edge of the line of swing points to the north. Do a quarter-turn, so that you're no longer facing the same way. And ask the pendulum for north again. If you think you know where north is, try to forget that – just let go, let the pendulum do it on its own without you trying to tell it what to do. And yes, I know it's rather like trying not to think about the word 'hippopotamus' . . . but just let go, let it be.

Another way is simply to point to the place. Think of your arm held out straight, with the index finger pointing away into the distance. Imagine, then, that your arm has an invisible extension, stretching out in a straight line to infinity. So that where that line touches the ground, or the wall, or the other side of the hedge, is 'here'. And that, as far as the pendulum is concerned, its response will occur when what you're looking for is at the place marked out by that invisible pointer, that invisible line.

So instantly you have X-ray vision: you can see through walls, see *inside* walls. In imagination only, of course: but you know how to *use* imagination with the pendulum to get useful results.

You can also find a specific spot by a kind of trigonometry, by finding the meeting point of two lines, two directions marked out by the response of the pendulum to your pointing. Let's say that you're trying to find where you dropped a ring in a field. Stand in one corner of the field and frame an instruction such as 'Give me a Yes when I'm pointing towards the ring.' Check first for an Idiot response – if so, the ring isn't in this field at all. Otherwise move your arm slowly round, covering the whole field. Note down where any response occurs. Then try again from another corner of the field. And, assuming that you had just one specific direction at each place, the point where the two lines cross is where you dropped the ring. We hope! With practice, though, you should be able to pinpoint small objects with surprising ease.

Another way of looking at things is to think of your hand not as a pointer but as an edge-detector. With the pendulum saying when to stop, move your hand forward, with the palm flat, to sense the edge of a field (or aura if you prefer). Try doing this round different people (assuming you can get them to co-operate – if not, try the cat). Imagine that there's a field of energy, an aura around them, describing the size of their life-force, their life-energy. (We don't have a clue what this aura might be, but it's a useful enough image; and anyway, I said *imagine* it, not try to work out what it 'really' is!) Start a few feet away from the person (or cat). With your palm flat and outstretched, like a policeman telling someone else to stop, walk towards them, telling the pendulum that you want it to respond, with a Yes or whatever, when your hand passes through the edge of this imaginary field. Or through the edges of it – there may be several layers to the field.

Several points to note here. One is to write your results down, and repeat them some other day, from time to time; but just note the changes, don't try to make them mean something. Meaning is something you'll learn as you go along – not from books! Another point is to note if you feel anything else in your hand at the point at which the pendulum says you've just met up with the edge of the field. A lot of people notice a tingling, rather like the static build-up around an over-stroked woolly sweater or plastic wrapping film, at that edge; other people notice a temperature change. Again, just note it, note how it changes with different people, or from day to day with the same people; don't try to make it fit some scheme of meaning. Instead, just observe. The pendulum only gives you a crude Yes/No answer: the total meaning you'll have to build up from what you observe. And, eventually, observe without needing the pendulum. But that, as they say, comes later.

A final pointing technique is probably the ultimate lazy man's guide to using the pendulum. Rather like a colleague who said that the way he avoids jet-lag is to get other people to come to see him, so that he doesn't have to travel at all, the trick here is to get other people to do your walking for you. Use them as markers, as pointers – the other end of an imaginary line from your eyes, marking the place that is 'here' as far as the pendulum is concerned. 'I am where that child is walking *now*': what could be easier? Imagine yourself being where that person is *now*.' Follow them. 'The leading edge of the leading foot' – except that it's that person's foot that you're using as the marker, not your own. Go back to that game we played in the last chapter, walking about in the street without having left your chair. Building a clear image of *being* there, without needing to be there in a physical sense at all. Yet in a sense this method is easier than imagination on its own, in that in a physical street you can see what's going on with your own eyes rather than only in your mind's eye; you can choose which one of many people to 'follow', to use as markers.

This method also has the nice advantage that you can hide in a car or a shop-doorway while your pendulum talks to itself under your guidance. So you don't have to get wet if it's raining. And you also avoid the potential embarrassment of wandering up and down the street earnestly watching the antics of this ball on a string!

IMAGINARY WORLDS

Go back to that game of walking about in an imaginary street. Imagine now looking down on it, from further and further above, until it becomes just a diagram, a map of the street and the area around it. Yet from there you can still, at the same time, imagine walking around in the street. Moving around on the map, you can move around in the street by looking at an image of the street.

So you can define 'here' as the place represented by a point on the map. Which means that you and your trusty pendulum can look for things represented by the details of the map. Note: not on the map – you know where that is, and there's nothing on the map's surface but ink and coffee-stains – but represented by the details of the map, as an image of the place that you want to look around. Images again.

The obvious advantage of map-dowsing is that you don't need to leave home. You can just look on the map, find things on the map. You can also move at impossible speeds – thousands of miles a second – and scan huge areas, all in one go, because it's all imaginary, all images. There's only one catch: you have to be good at imagining, to make those two places coincide in your mind: the 'here' that you're looking at on the imaginary world of the map, and the 'here' that you actually want to be looking at in the physical world.

That's not easy; in fact it's downright hard, and it takes a lot of practice to make it reliable. But that's all there is to it: you just wander around in an imaginary world, and make sure that that imaginary world coincides with the physical, 'objective' one.

Any image will do: a photograph; a diagram; even a rough sketch will do as long as you have enough information to hang your imagination on accurately. It doesn't even need to be a place: I've seen an electronic designer search with a pendulum for problems on a schematic diagram of a computer circuit. As long as you can make the image representative of the physical place or thing, in your own mind, you can wander around at will.

So: no problem about working with images. It's no different from what we've done before, defining 'here' as the place pointed to by your arm, for example: it's just that you have to be better at visualising where you would be if you were in the place represented by the image, because – unlike being out in the field – you have to see it with the mind's eye rather than your own eyes.

As for moving around within these worlds, there are plenty of techniques. In most of them you would point to the place with your fingers, or perhaps more precisely with a pin or some kind of pointer smaller than your finger.

For example, you can use a co-ordinate method, and scan down the side of the map, looking for a response when the horizontal line at that co-ordinate crosses over the position of the object; then do the same at the base of the map for a vertical co-ordinate; and where the two lines cross should be the position of the object. Not on the map, remember, but on the place represented by that point on the map.

Or you could use our original co-ordinate technique, and point out a direction (with a thread, perhaps) from two corners of the map to give you a final co-ordinate.

Or you could once again 'let your fingers do the walking' and just move your pointer over the map, letting the swing of the pendulum point out a direction to move in at each stage.

It's up to you.

But remember: it's only an imaginary world. Nothing is found, nothing is proven, until you have what you're looking for in your hand (assuming it is a thing you can actually hold in your hand). To do that, you have to find it in the field. Map-dowsing is a useful tool, an immensely powerful tool once you learn how to use it reliably: but it's never more than working on an image.

In effect, what you're doing in map-dowsing is asking the pendulum to tell you when the image of what you're looking for, which you've described in an imaginary way, coincides with the image of where you are on an image that is often a distinctly distorted image of where you want to look. And to get all these images to coincide with what's to be found in the physical world takes a real skill in mental acrobatics!

PLAYING FOR TIME

Our whole concept of time is imaginary. Time isn't a 'thing' that we can see or touch: we can experience it, but it slips past us even as we try to grasp it. Past and future aren't 'fact' at all, but are imaginary,

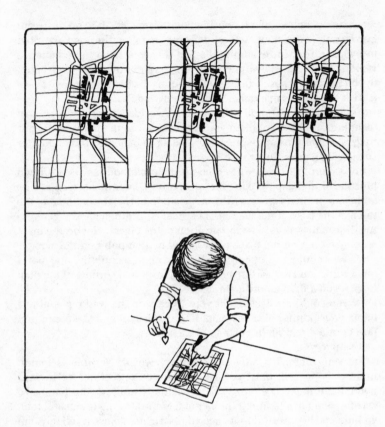

Map Dowsing Technique

images, gone or perhaps never to come. In a strict physical sense, there is only *now* and probability: the rest is guesswork in imaginary worlds, based on shadowy memories and our assumptions about future possibilities. Time is imaginary.

This is why working in time with the pendulum is no different from working on maps and diagrams. Both are entirely imaginary. And both take considerable skill and experience to improve the probabilities, the chances of getting anything useful out of them.

In principle it's easy enough. Let's say that you want to know what the water-flow of a stream was like last December. Easy enough: just use one of the quantitative techniques in conjunction with that question – 'Was the flow here last December greater than fifty gallons per minute?', for example. Just imagine that time as best you can. And because we have a sense of the past, of history, the pendulum's answer is likely to be accurate – with practice, of course. But ask what the flow's going to be like next December, and you can hit all sorts of problems: the best answer will only be a high probability of the actual amount of what you will be able to measure there when that time finally comes round.

Time is a maze of paradoxes. But everyone wants to play with prediction, where the effects of those paradoxes are most severe. As I say, in principle the techniques are the same as for map-dowsing, in that you have to define your position in time as well as in space, with 'here' being by default – in other words if you don't specifically define it as something else – here and now in a physical sense. But in practice it's not quite that easy: this is one technique that's best left until we look at applications in the next chapter.

TOOLS FOR 'WHICH HAVE I FOUND?'

We now have some basic tools to set up a meaning for that coincidence of what we're looking for and where we are. We have tools to define both. So now the pendulum has responded. Which response have we got? And what else do we need to know before that response is meaningful?

One question and its answer are rarely enough: we need to build up a picture out of the responses to a stream of questions. Not so much 'Here's an answer: so what was the question?' as 'Here's an answer: so what's the next question?', each answer leading to the next question to the next answer to the next question, until you've built up a detailed picture of what you're looking for, all built up out of Yes and No and a few quantities and directions.

So here we have tools and techniques both for what you might call 'follow-on' questions, and to direct the whole process of asking questions and receiving answers.

QUALITIES AND QUANTITIES

We know how to look for something with a pendulum. What's not so obvious is how to find out what you've got when you've found something that isn't quite what you were looking for.

One simple way, especially on outdoor work, is to try a number of samples at the spot, on the general lines of 'Is it this one?'. For water work, there's the Mager Disc I mentioned earlier. For anything else, you're back to inventiveness and native wit. Fishing for facts again. See what questions arise; follow up any of them, especially those that seem 'like a good idea at the time'. And see what response you get to each: in particular, watch out for Idiot responses, which can show you when you're on the wrong track.

For example, I remember in my early days I agreed to try to diagnose what was wrong with a small puppy. By using a stream of Yes/No questions looking at different parts of the body, I thought I had tracked it down to trouble in the liver: but from then on I got nothing but Idiot responses. Wrong question; unask the question. And I couldn't understand why; I couldn't work out what had gone wrong, or what to do next. It wasn't until later that I realised I had been looking for the root of the *symptoms*, not the trigger for those symptoms. The poor dog did indeed have liver trouble, but the root cause was intestinal worms! A few worming pills removed them *and* the liver problems.

Ask the right question, and the right answer arises. But miss a step somewhere in the sequence, and you and your pendulum will end up going round in circles very quickly! It's the same with any other form of analysis or scientific research: each question has to test just one part of each hypothesis, and the answer is then to be used to create the next question and the next hypothesis.

But where do the hypotheses come from? We soon learn that creating them is a skill in itself: but where does that skill come from? Good question; next question, says the scientist . . .

In dowsing, you're programming the responses of the pendulum, just as a computer's responses are programmed. As with a computer, changing the program is changing the rules, changing the context so that the same response can mean something different. And as in programming a computer, there are any number of ways of defining those rules, some of them good, many of them bad: 'good' and 'bad' being determined by how well they fit those criteria of 'efficient, reliable, elegant and appropriate'.

An example of this rule-changing is one of the routine 'follow-on' problems, namely finding the depth of what you've found. Here we first have to find the position of what we're looking for in one plane, the horizontal: then we have to find its position in the other plane, a vertical plane passing through the same spot. (If it isn't at that spot, watch out for an Idiot response when you look for its depth.)

So first find the position of the object – a coin, let's say. Walk around, using a question such as 'Give me a Yes when I'm standing directly above a coin.' Stop when you get the Yes response from the pendulum. You've now found the position in the horizontal plane: now you have to find out the depth of the coin.

The classic method is the so-called 'Bishop's Rule': 'distance out is distance down'. So first mark 'here' with a peg or something – tradition says an iron spike is best (though some dowsers would disagree, of course), but anything will probably do as long as you have something to come back to.

Now change the rules. You're still looking for the coin; but now you're looking for its depth, on the basis that distance out from 'here' until you get another response from the pendulum is the distance *down* to the coin from where you marked 'here'. Go back to 'here' and try again in a new direction, with the same rules set

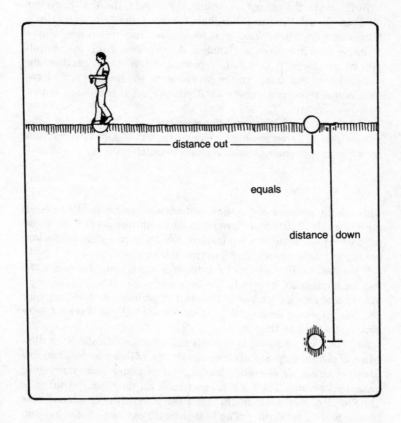

The Bishop's Rule

up: you should get the same response at the same distance out from 'here', even though it's in a different direction. If not, you've some thinking to do, of course!

Another way would be to walk on the spot – tread in place – at 'here', imagining that you're walking *downward* as you do so: the rules you'd change to in this case would be something like 'Give me a Yes when I've walked the same number of paces as I would if I were walking downwards.'

Or you could simply count: one turn of the pendulum in its Yes mode for each foot down, or each inch down, or whatever. You set the rules, so you can set the units that the rules follow too.

But perhaps the easiest method is, once again, the Yes/No system. You simply ask the pendulum how far down the coin is. Is it more than one foot down? Yes. Is it more than two feet down? No. Is it more than one foot six inches down? Yes. And so on until you've narrowed it down to a precise depth. Or – another way – decide on the units you're working in (inches, let's say) and then count through numbers until you get a Yes response: 'ten . . . twenty . . . thirty . . .'.

Watch out, though, for an Idiot response, which would mean that you've missed a step somewhere, or perhaps mistaken a No response for a Yes at some point – with obvious results!

YES AND NO AGAIN

This whole business of question and answer can be handled easiest with charts and lists and flowcharts, or anything else that gives you an ordered structure to keep track of what you're doing, where you are in the whole process. Back to ritual, if you like.

If you have a list, all you have to do is work your way down the list. Each question is there in the list – all you have to do is to point to each and check for a Yes or No. And, most important, to check for an Idiot response: because the list can't itself tell you if what you're looking for isn't on the list.

Any list. I've seen people use lists of homoeopathic and Bach remedies, of electronic parts, of cities and streets, of incenses for a magical ritual, of academic reference books. And, of course, any number of restaurant menus. There's even one book on dowsing (Jurriaanse's *The Practical Pendulum Book*) that consists mostly of charts and lists for use with a pendulum. The best lists, though, are those that *you* make up: the ones that match the way *you* work. Any list.

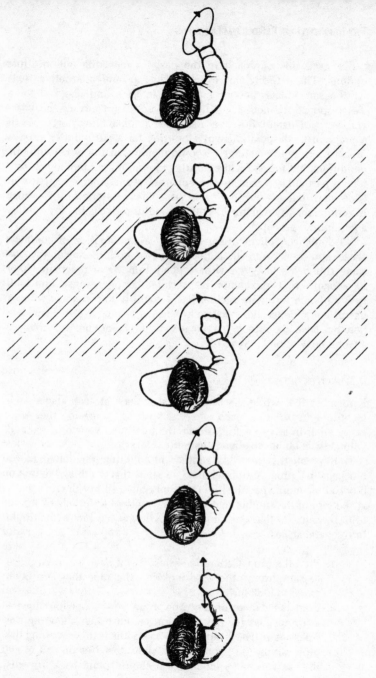

Finding a Pipe

I've used this approach in the past for checking out multiple options. The *I Ching*, for example, has several alternative texts for the same hexagram, so I pointed to each and checked for a Yes response. Sometimes I didn't get a Yes on any of the paragraphs: start again! But I've also used it on a flowchart plan of a program in desperation while hunting for a particularly elusive program error. Interestingly, I couldn't pick up the error with the pendulum, but instead while hunting I found myself looking closely for no particular reason at one apparently unconnected section of code: and that's where the error was. That was one of my earlier introductions to dowsing without a pendulum . . . using my eyes as a pendulum, perhaps?

No doubt you might prefer to call it a combination of common sense and luck. Agreed: actually there's no difference, it's the same thing. It's just that with a pendulum we're practising how to recognise that uncommon rarity called common sense; and luck isn't so much fortunate accident as the ability to recognise when a useful coincidence has occurred. And everything we've looked at here has been about tools to recognise useful coincidences – making a *technology* of luck, if you like.

KEEPING IT TOGETHER

Remember that while it's been easiest to look at each stage, each technique in isolation, each one of them has to work together with every other in a whole, to build up the totality of your practice and your skill. It all has to mesh together.

To illustrate this, let's take another outdoor example: looking for a blockage in a pipe. Assuming that you know that it's this pipe that is blocked, or more specifically is not only blocked but the one that's at the root of the trouble that you've been asked to fix (check for an Idiot response to that question, perhaps?), you can break this down into several stages:

1. Find the pipe. Generally easiest if you have a known place to start from; otherwise look for 'the pipe that I've been asked to look for'.
2. Find the course of the pipe. Here you're not looking for a 'thing', but for the direction of the thing: changing the rules again. The simplest way to do this is to walk along the pipe asking the pendulum to show the *direction* to move in – as you move off-course it should point back towards

the pipe, as we saw earlier in this chapter, in the section 'Pointing the way'.

3. At the same time as tracking the course of the pipe, you want to be looking for the blockage. One way to tackle this is to state that the pendulum should give a direction response continuously until you pass over the blockage, at which point it should gyrate, or do whatever else your Yes response happens to be. (That way you have a No or Idiot response as a warning of 'something else here'.)

4. At the site of the block, you need to find the depth. As you know, you have a wide variety of options here: count the depth, or use the old Bishop's Rule, or ask a series of 'How far . . .?' questions. Check that the depth you get isn't ridiculous: a drain-pipe isn't going to be more than a few feet down, so if you get a result in tens or hundreds of feet there's something wrong somewhere.

5. Then you need to check if there are *other* blocks – this may not be the only one.

All the time watch out for other things happening that might warn you if you're off the track somehow: absurd depths, or the pendulum quietly gyrating in answer to no particular question, for example, or a general sense – I can't think of any other way to describe it – that something's not what it should be.

That last, that combining of all the senses into a total synthesis, is what you need to develop most. In fact it can, even should, eventually replace your pendulum: reaching a stage where you *know*.

QUESTIONING THE ANSWERS

The totality of your sensing, merged into that synthesis, is your most powerful tool for questioning the answers that you receive. Your pendulum, which is you, is always willing to oblige you, and will be quite happy to give you false answers if that's what it thinks you want. (If you can't see why this should be so, think of the complexity of the psychology of blocks and prejudices, because that's what we're dealing with here.) Garbage in, garbage out, as the programmer would say. You *have* to have something else to counter that, to compare against, to contrast, to check. That something is called listening: discrimination; judgement; taste. Listening – active listening.

But using a pendulum, you're talking to the world, talking *at* the world. And the world is yourself, and everything inside and outside of you.

So you also need to listen. And it's not easy to listen while you're talking.

What you're listening for, or listening in, is the 'sound that is no-sound', or what the Zen student might describe as 'the sound of one hand clapping'.

You're looking for a space; a space in which things can happen. A quiet space: quiet, like fishing for facts, waiting for something to nibble at your line.

In a way trying to describe that state is like trying to describe that knack of balancing on a bicycle, or any other skill. Well, it's easy, you just balance: you know. Except that until you know what it's like in practice, you don't know; it doesn't make any sense. It just sounds like mystical mumbo-jumbo. Until you can ride the bicycle: then it's obvious. But then try to describe it to someone else, and you'll see how frustrating it is to try to put it into words! You know exactly what it is: except you can't say what it is. 'The Tao that can be told is not the eternal Tao': something like that. Another of the Joker's games, perhaps?

The pendulum follows a strict logic: you give it the rules, it gives you the answers according to the logic of the rules. *All* of the rules, as we've seen, including the ones that you're not aware that you've given it. But one of the severe, if not fatal, limitations of logic is that it can only answer *within* the framework of the rules: it has no means to question the rules at all.

The rules *are* the logic. So what makes the rules is outside logic; not illogical – that's easy, because that's just an absence of thought – but *alogical*. *Outside* logic. Beyond Yes-and-No thought.

Yes-and-No is about thinking, being focused, precise, asking one single unambiguous question at a time. But at the same moment we also need to be wide open, sensing everything, feeling for side-senses, warnings, mutterings, backgrounds, anything to balance the hard razor-like precision of thought. Working as a team, like the cameraman who can only see the world through the lens being balanced by the focus-puller who sees the world all around.

What we're talking about, then, is thinking narrow, being wide – at the same time. It's called listening; being.

We're looking for something, some way of working, some set of rules, that is efficient, reliable, elegant, appropriate. We could call it finding the technology of common sense. We could also call it finding the technology of you finding you.

THE ULTIMATE TOOLKIT

The ultimate toolkit is no toolkit at all. Or rather, it is a state in which you don't need individual tools, individual techniques. Instead, you *are* them, all of them, at the same time.

Now this calls for a very impressive degree of skill in mental acrobatics, in sensing, in selecting which tool and technique to be at any moment, always choosing the most appropriate tool. We would call it perfection, mastery. But we've both a long way yet to go before we get to that place!

6 • PUTTING IT INTO PRACTICE

Now that we've worked our way through that lot, we may have a better answer to the question with which we ended the previous chapter – namely, what's the use? Because all those tools and techniques we looked at are only useful when we put them to use.

That's up to you, of course. You'll need to find your own way, your own applications. But what I can do here is make some suggestions of places to start, some basic approaches to try, to see what you want to do with the pendulum – if anything, of course!

Two things to remember though. First, the pendulum is a surprisingly versatile tool, but as I've said before it is *not* a substitute for thinking. I've known people who could not decide on anything without first consulting their beloved pendulum. Now while this might be a useful exercise for a short while, it can also be a dangerous addiction: if you get into that state and then lose your pendulum, you will have quite literally lost your mind. It's a tool, not a requirement: never let yourself become so fascinated by it that you *need* it!

And second, another reminder that the pendulum is only one tool among many, not the whole toolkit. It handles some questions easily and well, questions such as 'Is it here?'; but for some other questions, like 'What do I do now?', it's often worse than useless. In a way talking about the pendulum is rather like talking about different types of hammer: you can do some surprising things with a hammer, but if you give one to a child it will think everything needs hammering. We used to nickname the hammer 'the Birmingham screwdriver' because mechanics seemed to think that that's what you should use to put screws in with – but there *are* better tools in the toolkit for that job!

Efficient, reliable, elegant, appropriate: a useful set of guidelines – together with another acronym: 'KISS'. Short for 'Keep it simple, Sunshine!'

In short, keep thinking. At the same time, keep sensing. Thinking narrow; being wide.

BACK TO THE PARLOUR

Perhaps the best place to start putting it all into practice is back in the parlour. Playing games again.

This time, however, we're playing games in which we actually want results. Although we may say (mainly to keep the Joker at bay) that it doesn't have to work, it would certainly be nice if it did. Boost morale and all that.

One minor point, though. Don't try too hard; don't push it. Using a pendulum is often a little like driving in fog: every sense is straining for any information out of the mass of nothingness up ahead. As a result, it can be tiring: the harder you try, and the longer you keep hammering at it, the more tiring it gets. So don't. Do it in easy stages. Just play!

CAR KEYS

We played hunt-the-thimble earlier: now we're going to play the same game in earnest. You've lost your car keys. Now how do you find them?

You can't start with the question of 'Where are my keys?'. Because the pendulum will probably answer Yes. Helpful as ever. You need to be more specific than that.

So define what you're looking for. Visualise the keys, build an image of them. They're *my* car keys. For *this* car. With a key-ring that looks like this. And I need to find them, please. Now! Because I'm late already . . .

But don't panic: let go, let it happen by itself. See what else arises, what other information comes to mind while you're using the pendulum.

First question: are they in the house?

Assuming that the answer's Yes (otherwise you'll have to work it out on your own), we now have to break the search down to smaller and smaller areas.

Are they upstairs? Or downstairs? (Watch for an Idiot response.)

Are they in this room?

Ask the pendulum to point out the direction to the keys. Follow along the line that it points; state in your mind that you want the pendulum to go round in a Yes mode when you're over them. Leading edge of the leading foot.

The pendulum still hasn't given a Yes, but you've walked up to the coat-rack. You've already searched there: you know they're not in your jacket-pocket. I think . . . that's where they should have been, that's where they were last I remember . . .

No, not in my jacket pocket. Stupid pendulum. Why bother? Wait a moment – it's started to go round, though. Why?

Point to each coat in the rack. It's stopped going round now: no yes for any of them.

Back off a bit. And now it's going round again. Nearer the floor. Useless.

Hang on, though – I remember hearing something drop when I put my jacket away last time.

All right then, check the boots on the floor.

Here they are! They'd fallen inside this boot!

I must have known it all along – all I had to do was think about it a little. Didn't need the pendulum anyway, did I? After all, it's only coincidence . . .

MAN-HUNT

Another game: a paper-chase without the paper, a man-hunt chasing an imaginary trail.

You'll need at least two people for this, at somewhere like a park or a piece of woodland with a number of trails.

First, one of you should go off into the distance, taking any route. It's probably a good idea to agree to meet up with the others somewhere in, say, half an hour: until then, hide.

Then wait a minute or so: then they have not only to find you, but also to identify the route you took.

Your turn to search. She's gone; the minute's up. Time to start looking.

You're looking for her. Build an image of her. If you can't visualise her face – that's often surprisingly difficult – try sneaking up on her from behind, so to speak: build an image of the back of her head, recall the way she walks, her typical stances. If you have something of hers at hand – her sweater, for example – use it as a sample of her as well: 'This is who I'm looking for. And I'm looking for her now.'

Ask the pendulum for the initial direction. Not where she is now – she may well have moved round – but the direction she started off in. Remember that you want to find the route she took as well as where she is now.

Follow that path. At each junction, check with the pendulum; but also look for any confirming clues, like the pattern of her shoe-print in the track. The pendulum (which is you) will be seeing those as well: but it should help if you see them too.

Watch out at junctions if the pendulum swings in both directions: she may well have taken both paths at different times while she was hiding, just to confuse you. Throw you off the scent, so to speak. If that's the case, tell the pendulum to follow her path in sequence.

Keep your mind on the idea that you're looking for her. Don't get distracted by the fact that it's a sunny day, or that there are some interesting things around here: you're looking for the route she took. Here. Now. Nothing else.

Try it, without trying.

And if you don't find her this time, well, it's only practice. You'll meet up in half an hour; then you can try again.

It's an interesting game, though, and one that does have practical applications. I've known a few dowsers who specialise in 'missing persons' cases, for example. But if you want to follow this up, do be aware of the ethics of the game: some so-called 'missing persons' don't want to be found, and have every right and need to retain their privacy!

PLACE YOUR BETS

We all need more money. You say the pendulum can answer questions: so which horse is going to win the three o'clock at Haydock Park? Here's the list of runners . . .

Sorry, but it isn't quite that simple!

If you try the 'place your bets' game too seriously you'll run up against the paradoxes of prediction: you will at best only get the most likely future as can be seen at the present time, which is no better than you'd get by studying the racing form in the time-honoured way. And besides, the Joker seems to take particular enjoyment in playing nasty tricks – expensive nasty tricks at that – on people who think that they can bend the rules of chance indefinitely for personal gain.

But 'place your bets' is a useful parlour game to play, because it's a good example with which to practise dowsing in time. So play it: but with the emphasis on play . . .

Get today's newspaper, and select a suitable race: the three o'clock at Haydock Park will do just fine.

Select the list of runners. It might be a good idea to cut it out of the newspaper, or even to copy it onto another sheet of paper, simply to focus your attention on it: in the same way as it's often easier to remember something if you write it down.

This race; these horses; these jockeys.

Is this horse going to run today? Will it be first past the post? Will it be last? (You could have a side-bet on that too.) Take care not to confuse its position, its number past the post, with its race-number. And remember that you're after its position past the *winning*-post – not any old post somewhere on the course.

Frame the whole question clearly in your mind, without stray ambiguities.

Go right through the list. The same questions for each horse on the list.

Before the race, do the whole thing all over again. For each horse; for each jockey. Keep your mind on the job: these horses, this race. Note if there's any difference. There may well be changes: one of the horses may have been withdrawn from the race. On the other hand, there may be no change. Either way, note it down.

And do the same *after* the race: you're not looking for a prediction now, but looking for information about what has happened. You're looking in the past, not the future: the race is over, you want the result. Note if any seem to have pulled out of the race. Note if any horses finished without their riders (it does happen).

And later in the day, check up on the published results. Then curse me for warning you not to place any money on it, when you discover you had it right all along!

So next time you do it, you place money on it: you got it dead right last time, so it'll work perfectly this time. Obviously.

It's so obvious, so certain, that it'll work perfectly. But it doesn't. Don't be surprised if not a single one of your predictions turns out right; you'll probably lose every bet you placed. And perhaps *that's* when you'll understand what I've been trying to tell you about the Joker. Don't say I didn't warn you!

WATER, WATER EVERYWHERE

Most people seem to think of the dowser as a water-diviner: some aged and bearded countryman with a forked hazel rod coming to life in his hands as he passes over an underground stream. It's a nice image: nostalgic rather than realistic though. Because what you're doing with a pendulum is dowsing: you're learning to be a dowser. And you don't even need a forked stick.

But perhaps you'd better know something about water-divining, just to keep people happy. You don't want to spoil their illusions, do you?

Actually it's still an important part of dowsing, and one that will continue to be so: we'll always need more water. Yet those infamous television pundits will no doubt insist that it's no more than a historical aberration now entirely superseded by science, in the form of geology. To an extent, from their viewpoint, that's true: geology has improved a little over the past few centuries. But while geologists do know a great deal about some areas, they know surprisingly little about others. And in any case geology is a poor predictive tool in places where the underground structures are a mess, as in Somerset in England or the earthquake country of California.

Geology deals with areas, shapes, relationships, patterns – which is fine if you want to know the general layout of a place, but not much use if you need to know exactly what is where. If that's what you need, you either have to dig a hole and hope that you've hit the right spot, or you call in an experienced dowser first. Because dowsing is a form of perception, designed to notice *change*, it's not so good on generalities, continuities: but it *is* good on details.

And if you're looking for water, here, on *this* farm, it's details you want. Not 'there might be some water somewhere round here, if you're lucky, perhaps'; but Yes. Or No. Precisely.

Serious water-finding is a serious business: a frightening amount of money and in many cases quite a few livelihoods and even lives depend on you getting it right. There are professional water-dowsers in every country, many of them working on the basis of 'no water, no pay' – and that includes the horrendous cost of the borehole, which may go down hundreds of feet to a precise point. So they have to get it right. And they do. But as with any skill, there's an awful lot to learn, an awful lot of things that can go wrong; not at all trivial.

That kind of water-divining is really outside the scope of this book (if you want to learn more, the old master-apprentice system is still the best: contact one of the national dowsers' societies, they'll put you in touch with an experienced member). But there are plenty of less risky variations on the theme that are useful around the house – or farm, for that matter – such as finding where pipes and cables and drains have been laid. And for that we do already have the tools.

PIPES AND CABLES

You could argue that we also have other tools already for that kind of job: metal-detectors, for example. True: but have you actually *used* one yourself? They're fine if what you're looking for is a few inches down and clearly distinguishable from everything else. But you may have noticed that builders like making their pipe-trenches deep, to protect them from frost and the occasional wayward child with a spade: and to use even the most modern ultrasonic 'metal-detector' (more accurately, 'discontinuity detector') to find a plastic water-pipe three feet down in amongst the usual buried building-site rubbish demands an awareness and discrimination – to separate 'signal' from background 'noise' – not much different from that you need for using a pendulum for the purpose.

Anyway, the pendulum's cheaper.

There are, of course, some trade-offs. Your pendulum is equally reliable – and unreliable – regardless of distance: it depends on you, on your skill. But the reliability of physical tools like the metal detector depends on physical rules that say that the signal-strength only gets weaker as the distance increases, which means that they may well be more reliable than the pendulum if distances are small. And there are other considerations to think about, such as safety. So if it's a live power-wire that you're looking for, an inch or two inside a wall, *do* use a metal detector: it's safer. There's no point in risking getting a shock for the sake of a minor practical experiment. On the other hand, if you'd have to dig up half the garden anyway to find the break in a drainpipe, you may as well use the pendulum first. If you don't find it with the pendulum you can always return to the old brute-force-and-ignorance method: and it won't have cost you anything but a little time and some useful experience.

Anyway, let's assume that you're looking for a water-pipe that has a suspected break in it. The principle's the same for drains and cables, but let's use a feed-pipe as an example.

You want to fix the break.

First, find your pipe.

Obviously it helps if you know where to start: if you know where it enters the house, for example. If you do, then do something to say that it's *this* pipe that you're looking for: tie a handkerchief on it, perhaps. *This* pipe.

Or you could find it on a map of the house, such as an architect's plan. Beware, though: the plan may say where the pipes were *supposed* to be, but that doesn't necessarily mean that the builders bothered to put them there.

If you don't know where it starts, build up an image of it: if you have something suitable as a sample for the pipe, use it. You could even take a sample of the water from the outlet, and use that as a sample. Anything goes: it's up to you.

Walk round the house with your sample. You're looking for a Yes response when you walk over the pipe: the leading edge of the leading foot marks 'here'. Note any Idiot or, particularly, No responses: they may be other pipes or cables, not the one you're looking for, but may be useful later none the less.

When you get a Yes response, keep going, then turn round and come back. Check if you get the same place. Don't be surprised if it's not the same: beginners often overshoot. Remember too to come back over the spot as if you've never been there before in your life: watch out for the old booby-trap of 'I got a response there last time so I ought to get the same there again'. The whole point of re-crossing the place is to *check*, not to tell yourself what you already know!

Make sure you're clear as to what you're looking for: it's *that* drainpipe. Is that the pipe that's here: this one?

Once you're satisfied that you've found some part of the pipe, we can start to look along it for a break.

FINDING THE BREAK

To some extent you should know how to do this already – we used it as an example in the last chapter.

The principle's the same as it was then: except now you're doing it for real. Or at least you should be.

We've changed the rules. So far we've been looking only for the pipe; now we're looking not only for its direction, but also for any breaks in the continuity of the pipe: a change, something different.

Obviously you can go two ways at this point: upstream as far as the flow (if any) is concerned, or downstream. So start off by using the pendulum to decide which way to go. Swing the pendulum in Neutral, and ask it to point out the direction to go in. Watch the *front* edge of the swing: it should move to the left or right, still swinging backwards and forwards in a kind of neutral but pointing out a direction. (Refer back to the previous chapter if you're not sure of what techniques to use here.)

Now set the rules: the pendulum should not only point out the direction but should give a Yes response when you're passing over a break. Set up a side-rule that a No should mean 'something else interesting but not a break as such' – a branch in the pipe, perhaps. (Keep the Idiot response in reserve to tell you when you're completely off track – checking the wrong pipe, for example.)

Follow the line that the pendulum gives as a direction. Keep in mind that you want to follow *this* pipe, and that you want the pendulum to continue to point out the direction to go in to follow it. And also that you're looking for a break, a discontinuity in the pipe, leakage.

It's quite probable that you'll find yourself zig-zagging around a little, overshooting the pipe slightly each time you cross it. Remember not to try too hard, though!

And now: a Yes response.

Mark the place: find a twig or a piece of bark, or kick your heel into the ground or something like that. And keep moving along the pipe. There may be more than one break. I've known more than one pipe that bore a distinct resemblance to a sieve when we finally uncovered it!

You've been looking for the break. And now that you've apparently found it (or them): the proof. Which means, of course, that you now have to start digging!

HOW DEEP? HOW MUCH?

Digging is all you have to do for a break in a pipe. (Agreed, you have to mend the break too – but that's hardly a dowsing problem, is it?) If you missed the right place – well, you would have had to dig up the lawn anyway. The pendulum saves a little time, but isn't essential: the main point here is that it's good practice on something for which it's useful but not critical that you get it right.

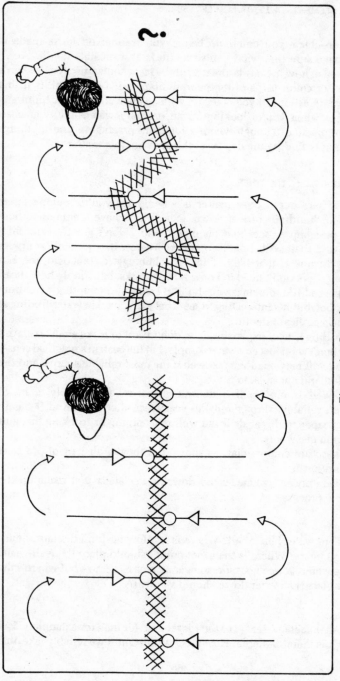

Zig-zagging Over the Pipe

One check you could do before you wander off for a spade is to make sure that what you've found is at a sensible depth. We've looked at how to do this already, in the last chapter: use the 'Bishop's rule', or count turns of the pendulum, or ask a stream of 'Is it *this* deep?' questions. If you come up with an answer in tens or hundreds of feet when you're looking for an ordinary water-pipe, you need more practice! Though whether it's more practice in finding things or simply finding the depths of things is another matter.

LINKING IT ALL TOGETHER

But where depth does matter is when what you're looking for *is* tens or hundreds of feet down. (No, I don't have a clue as to how it's possible to 'see' that far down, and I don't greatly care: all I know is that, with practice and experience, it *is* possible – unless you assume that it isn't. This is technology, a 'practical art', not science. We don't need to know how it works, but simply how it can be worked.) At this stage you shouldn't even be attempting something like that, but it's interesting to see what's involved in water-finding at some significant depth.

Drilling is very expensive. You don't want to make a mistake. And you don't want just any water-supply, but the best: in a practical sense, a trade-off between the most water, the most reliable source, and the easiest and cheapest to get to.

A well is useless if it doesn't give a reliable supply: a lot of water, reliably, throughout the year, year after year. And it has to be cheaper to dig or drill the well than piping or trucking the stuff in from elsewhere.

These are commercial decisions: but they're all part of practical water-finding.

There are, of course, many dowsing decisions that make up the whole process.

Where
Is there water here at all? Where is it? How far from the farm-house or the fields? Where is the *exact* point I should place the well-shaft? (The water-source may spread over an area or a line – but where's the *best* place?) How far down should we drill?

What
Is it drinkable water? (Try the Mager Disc for that, for example.) How much is there available? How much water could we reliably take out?

When

How much water is there available now? How much in the dry season last year? How much in a typical year? How much is there likely to be in a bad year? How much are we likely to get (not 'How much *will* we get?') next December?

Questions, questions. All of them phrased in an unambiguous way, clear, precise.

Ask a woolly question and you'll get a woolly answer. Ask a clear question and you'll get a clear answer. Even if it's one you don't like.

Remember that the water-finder is another engineer: someone who has to produce results. Or tell you, in advance, that there aren't any useful results to be had. Plenty to be had in an imaginary world, perhaps, of nice things happening nicely just at the right time: but not necessarily in the dust and sweat of the desert or the back end of Berkshire. Reality, the objective world we and the rest of the world live in, doesn't always do what we'd like it to, doesn't always (or doesn't often) match up to how we imagine it could be: but that's how it is.

PLAYING WITH FOOD

We can also, all too easily, imagine a world in which everything goes wrong: and strangely enough, the world's only too happy to oblige you in that.

This is another area where I get cross with the way some people play with a pendulum. You can easily make the world a great deal worse for yourself, simply by taking the pendulum's answers too literally. Taking games too seriously. And the best (or perhaps worst) example is playing with food.

The pendulum can be a very useful tool to help you to develop an intuitive understanding of how different kinds of food and drink affect you. But it's really sad to watch cases where the tool has taken over: to see someone who's become obsessed with the use of the pendulum, expecting the pendulum to do their thinking for them. I can remember on several occasions watching an old lady in a café: having bought a cup of coffee, she'd then pull out her crystal pendulum from her handbag to see whether it considered the coffee safe for her to drink. If she'd done this *before* buying the coffee, perhaps . . . but no, the pendulum hadn't remembered to do that for her, so she hadn't thought of asking the question. The pendulum had the last word. It decided everything about her life. After all, it was divinely guided, it knew so much more about everything than she did . . .

This is crazy! But it's also depressingly common.

So let's go over it all once more. The pendulum isn't apart from you, but a part of you. You tell it what to do: it shows you the answers accordingly. Which you give to it to show you. So you already know all the answers: it's just that it's not easy to see them at first. So the pendulum is a tool to tell you what you know already. And since you already knew it, you don't actually need the pendulum in the first place.

The pendulum is *not* a substitute for thinking. It's a tool, a crutch, to help you to learn how to *know*. Nothing more. A useful tool, sure. So let's use it, and not let *it* use *us* – which *would* be crazy.

COFFEE-TIME

Having been rude about that old lady, I'm now going to suggest that you do exactly the same. Just plain awkward, I suppose. But there is an important difference: you're doing this as an exercise, whilst she did it as a way of life.

So let's have a cup of coffee, like the old lady. In fact it's probably worth taking a break now anyway.

Coffee-time. Coffee is a kind of occupational hazard for a computer programmer; I suppose it must be for many other trades as well. Each time I get frustrated with what I'm writing, or get stuck while disentangling some piece of program code, I'll go and make another cup of coffee for myself and my colleagues. And since they do the same, we seem to get through gallons of the stuff. So surely it can't be all that good for us?

Let's use the pendulum to find out. *Strictly* as an exercise, though.

I feel like having yet another cup of coffee. I'll assume you want one too. And that you want to use the pendulum to tell you what to put in it. So:

'Black or white?'

– to which, of course, the answer is Idiot. It's an ambiguous question: an answer of Yes or No wouldn't make sense. So unask the question; rephrase the question.

'Should I have milk in this cup of coffee?'

In my case the answer's often No: I overdose on milk rapidly. But let's assume that the answer's Yes.

Ask the pendulum to 'say when': holding the milk carton, pour the milk slowly until the pendulum says No.

If the cup's overflowing at this point, you haven't been taking enough care over your dowsing practice!

The next question is how much sugar. Or sweetener, if you must. Use a counting technique, remembering to check for a possible answer of None; or perhaps, as with the milk, keep pouring the stuff in until the pendulum tells you to stop.

Now comes the proof: drinking the result.

If it's revolting – well, it's called 'eating your words'. (Fair enough, 'drinking your words' would be more accurate, but it doesn't sound right.) The pendulum gave you the answers you asked for: it said what you told it to say. Perhaps what it's really trying to tell you is that you've had quite enough coffee already today, but you didn't get round to asking that question!

READING THE MENU

Another example of this game is reading a menu in a restaurant: using the pendulum to choose what you're going to have to eat, with the proof of your skill with the pendulum being literally in the eating!

The menu is a list of options. And you know how to use a pendulum with a list. Just point to each entry on the list, and see which ones you get a Yes for: make up a short-list, so to speak. 'Would this most suit my appetite today?'

If you don't end up with a short-list of one, go through the list again. In particular, note the varying degrees of Yes (and No) that you can see on the pendulum. For some items on the menu the pendulum will give a kind of 'Well, not too bad' or 'might be all right'; see if you get a definite Yes for anything.

If you don't get any kind of Yes for anything, perhaps it's time to change restaurants.

Do remember, though, that this is an *exercise*. It's not something you *have* to do. And it's probably not that good an idea to make it too public: it might be all too quick a method of insulting the management. Which is perhaps why the pendulum kept on giving you Idiot responses to everything!

In other words, it's a game. Keep it that way.

There are a few occasions, though, where it can be a practical game. You'll often find that foreign restaurants assume a perfect familiarity with the language, and don't bother with such trivialities as an explanation of what their dishes are. So you're faced with 'rojan ghosh' or 'bhindi bhajee' or something that vaguely translates as 'flowers of the sky' – and you haven't a clue as to what they are. So what do you choose?

This is where the pendulum becomes useful, or at least interesting. In this instance you *don't* know what the 'right' answer would be: you're reduced to guessing. So you may as well make it inspired guesswork, and use the pendulum to increase the inspiration. And if what you end up with is raw squid or bears a close resemblance to char-grilled shoe-leather – well, perhaps you needed to find out what it tasted like, if only to know that you wouldn't want to taste it again!

WEIGHT-WATCHING

Another example of where pendulum-waving in a restaurant really can be of some practical value is when you're watching your weight. Since you don't know what's going to be in what you're about to order, that book of calorie values isn't actually going to be much use: you haven't a clue as to what the calorie count of that dish would turn out to be.

So instead you can use the pendulum. 'Does this dish have the least calories?' – something like that. Or use a counting technique along with a question such as 'What's the calorie count for this dish?'

Or perhaps, since you know perfectly well that the salad is the one with the least calories but you don't want yet *another* salad for lunch, you could use 'Does this (excluding the salad) have the least calories?'. In other words you can select out certain items: to return to the radio analogy, you're defining what is to be interpreted as signal and what is noise, so that you can, if you like, *pre-declare* that something – in this case the salad – is to be ignored as 'noise'.

Something else that's hard about weight-watching is the discipline of it all. Resisting temptation – again and again and again. Perhaps you don't have to. You could, for example, set yourself a target and use the pendulum to check everything you eat, to tell you when you've reached that target and have to stick to limp lettuce for the rest of the day. As with coffee-time, use the pendulum to tell you when to stop pouring the cream.

But – once again – *don't* let this use of the pendulum become a way of life. It's a tool. Not the answer. And in the case of weight-watching, a tool to reinforce your own discipline, and *not* the discipline itself. Sorry, but it's your weight you're trying to limit, not the pendulum's: and if it (which is, of course, you) thinks that you'd be happiest ploughing through an entire plateful of cream cakes – which might well be true – well then it's quite likely to oblige, and advise you accordingly. Which won't help you reduce weight: quite the opposite, in fact.

The pendulum isn't a substitute for thinking; and it's not a substitute for the will to resist those greedies. That's up to you, too. It's a cruel world. . .

REACTIONS AND ALLERGIES

Another cruel reality is that all too often the things we most like to eat turn out to be things we're actually allergic to, even if only mildly so. (In my case, it's milk products, especially ice cream and certain soft cheeses.) Perhaps we like them because the body's reaction gives us a kind of buzz: I don't know. All I know is that for me a large ice cream at lunch-time equals an afternoon of wandering around half-asleep with sore lips and a very full feeling in my stomach – and I love the stuff! Cruel indeed.

All of us are allergic to something; and it usually doesn't matter in the slightest that we are. To my mind far too many people spend far too much of their time panicking about allergies: but why bother? You could even say that we're allergic to living, since in the end we all die of it.

All right, so I shouldn't be so cynical. It often does matter. But we've all seen people who would drive anyone crazy: 'Oh no, I couldn't touch that, it might possibly have seen a cow in a past incarnation' – that sort of rubbish. Overgrown children picking at their food as a childish way of grabbing attention: we don't need to encourage that, surely?

Anyway, I accept that it does matter on occasion: seriously so, in the case of people with some illnesses such as diabetes. And even if it's not serious, it can be an annoyance: I can't get much work done if I'm half-knocked-out by some of those cheeses I love. And it's especially difficult to spot potential problems in a restaurant, or for that matter at a party, when you don't know what's in the food or drink. Especially as some substances only cause us trouble when they're together with other specific things. So here again we can use the pendulum to get us to tell us in advance when there's likely to be something which we may like but which doesn't much like us.

It's much the same sort of question as we used in the restaurant, but with a slightly different slant: 'Is this good for me?', for example. Beware of the old double-negative question – 'Is this bad for me?' – in which No can mean negative (it is bad) or false (it isn't bad, therefore possibly good). Again it doesn't matter what the nominal 'cause' of a problem might be: all you need to know is that you want to avoid any problems at all. So it isn't a case of avoiding mushrooms or monosodium glutamate or whatever, but simply avoiding trouble.

Then again, you do have to eat . . .

To take another approach, something that you're sure may cause you problems may well be beneficial under other circumstances: it's often not a particular substance that's a problem, but the *amount* of that substance. Within a certain range – even of known toxins – there'll be no trouble: after all, that's how homoeopathic remedies are believed (if that's the right word) to work. So you could use the pendulum while cooking, to select different ingredients, different flavourings, even different timings, with the pendulum doing a simple 'say when' trick much as we did with the milk in the coffee earlier – remembering, or course, not to take the whole thing too seriously.

Try it. If you get it wrong from time to time, well, you'll feel the effects – perhaps. Perhaps not. As I say, it usually doesn't matter. But it's an interesting exercise anyway, to use the pendulum to get you to tell you what you should and shouldn't be eating – and how much, too.

And, as before, the proof is in the eating. Good luck!

PHYSICIAN, HEAL THYSELF

Healing is an emotive subject. Not surprising, really, when its effects – or lack of them – have a major impact on our everyday lives. But there's probably been more utter rubbish said and written about healing and medicine than any other subject in history – from every tradition of medicine, mainstream or 'alternative'.

One thing I did learn from an upbringing in a medical household is that while medical science (such as it is) has much to say about why people fall ill, it has almost nothing to say about why they don't. And still less about why people fall well: you can almost hear the complaint that it isn't scientific, that people shouldn't be allowed to get better on their own if it can't be explained. Something like that, anyway.

But as we've already seen, things don't have to 'fit' somebody else's rules, fortunately; but also unfortunately – sometimes it's worth keeping to the rules. Because any form of medicine can work: and it can just as easily work to the detriment of the long-suffering patient as well as to their benefit.

Any form of healing is legal in Britain – at present. In some other countries, though, it's not that simple (I'll avoid using the term 'free'). In the States, for example, the American Medical Association and the drug companies have a virtual stranglehold on medicine: it's illegal for anyone other than a licensed doctor or, in some cases, a priest, to diagnose or prescribe any form of treatment for any form of disease. But in some ways that's not that bad: it does at least restrict the damage-makers to the mainstream end of the profession – though they certainly cause damage enough.

The problem is that curative medicine is fun, glamorous. You can see the results. You did it. Or at least you can claim the credit for it. Preventive medicine, on the other hand, is boring: the whole idea is that nothing happens. But unfortunately the best preventive medicine is often to leave things alone. To use an engineer's adage, 'If it don't need fixin', don't fix it!'

I remember one dowsing conference where various people were running around almost desperately trying to 'heal' others, whether they wanted healing or not, and always with exaggerated poses and expectations of gratitude. By the end of this unfunny farce most of us were left feeling distinctly ill – but the 'healers' were noticeably healthier! It reminded me of the laconic comment used all too often in surgeons' reports in the early nineteenth century: 'Operation successful, but patient died.' Which seems a somewhat extreme example of missing the purpose of medicine.

So one useful watchword is the old phrase 'Physician, heal thyself.' *Thyself* – you. Not others: you. Practise on yourself first before attempting to tell others what to do. When you're perfect, perhaps you have the right to meddle in other people's well-being: until then, you don't have that right. Certainly not if they haven't asked you for help, at any rate.

Physician, heal *thyself*. Before you can honestly work on others, you need to have a better understanding of yourself. And one way of doing that is to use the pendulum to help in looking at yourself and your interaction with the world.

FINDING THE REMEDY

One popular starting-place is the Bach remedies, a collection of thirty-eight basically herbal mixtures which supposedly treat states of mind: depression, loneliness, over-excitedness and the like. They're intended to be used on your own, by you, for you, rather than for inflicting on others; and their one great advantage is that they do appear to be harmless if mis-prescribed. Perhaps, as some would argue, that's because they don't do anything at all. Maybe they do, maybe they don't: as usual, the theory doesn't matter, but the experience does.

So for the next game (which you don't have to play, of course) you'll need a set of Bach remedies. They're sold in little bottles at health food stores or specialist suppliers, either individually or as a set (usually together with descriptive leaflets): otherwise borrow a set from a friend. Lay them out in front of you. All of them – like the keys of a piano – with the labels facing away from you. The idea now is to go through them with the pendulum to find which one, or several, most approximates to your state of mind today. Use a question such as 'Would this be appropriate for my needs today?'

Go through the entire set. For some bottles you'll get a definite Yes; for some bottles you'll get an equally definite No. Others will give you at most a kind of 'nothing much' response, with the pendulum perhaps drifting slightly away from Neutral as if vaguely interested in what's going on. Note down all the responses, including the 'nothing much' ones.

Now turn the bottles round, and compare your Yes and No responses with the descriptions on the labels. Anything interesting?

An experiment you might like to do (at your own risk, says my publisher!) is to use the remedies in accordance with the pendulum's comments that you've just noted down: perhaps one drop of each bottle that gave you a Yes response, or else get the pendulum to tell you how many drops to use. Come back a couple of hours later: note if you perceive any difference in your mental state. It's perhaps not easy to see any difference, though, since you're always seeing the world through those changing states.

As an exercise, repeat this sequence of test-and-dose once a day for perhaps a week. Keep a diary for that week: note down your moods, your attitude of mind. Observe how you observe what's going on. (This is actually the real version of what's called 'being scientific', but don't let that worry you.) Using the pendulum to help you in looking at yourself and your interaction with the world.

FOR MY NEXT TRICK ...

The Bach remedies are relatively cheap, but they still cost money. So why not make up a list and use that, you say? Exactly. You can. Just find a list of the remedies and go down it with a pointer, noting the pendulum responses. You've been using the remedies for long enough that you can imagine them clearly, can build a clear image of each bottle and its label and its contents.

And you then discover that you can *imagine* taking the respective dose too, and find that it has exactly the same effect as taking it from the physical bottle. An imaginary medicine – but with real effects.

This is where things start to get distinctly strange.

Mainstream medicine assumes that things work according to the normal assumptions of mainstream science. In this view, the body is merely a collection of interlinked but separate parts, making up a complex piece of plumbing and chemical engineering. Any chemical, suitably applied, will have a known, predictable effect. We assume 'more is more': to create more of an effect, you use a bigger dose of the chemical. Except that even in mainstream medicine this doesn't always work: things have, as usual, all sorts of exceptions and side-effects and ifs and buts and perhaps, until you realise that it doesn't bear much resemblance to what we're told is science at all. And there is this strange problem called the 'placebo effect', where a dummy drug (used as a 'control' in clinical trials) turns out to work well for a significant percentage of patients. And since the same dummy drug – typically calcium lactate, a kind of chalky sugar – is used in trials for totally different 'real' drugs, it seems that the dummy could be used, in a sense, to 'treat' virtually *any* disease.

Then we have homoeopathy, whose basic principles are exactly the opposite: the body can only be seen as a whole, and 'less is more', in that the more diluted the substance is, the more powerful it gets. Or rather that at greater dilutions some kind of 'essence' is increased or emphasised. Although most common homoeopathic remedies are diluted a thousand or a million times (marked as '3X' or '6X'), in some cases the dilutions are so extreme (such as '200X', or 10^{-200}) that it's unlikely, statistically speaking, that there's a single molecule of the original drug in the entire bottle, let alone the little droplet you take on a lump of sugar: and yet it still works. All that's left, so to speak, is the essence or idea of the original substance: literally, something imaginary. And it's that 'something imaginary' that does the work. Why it works or how it works is totally beyond our comprehension: yet experience tells us that it *does* work.

Getting better coincides with the use of the remedy, whether it be a 'real' drug, a dummy, or something that's little more than an idea. In a sense, then, it's entirely coincidence and mostly imaginary. But haven't we seen that phrase somewhere before?

We're back at that paradox of 'Things have not only to be seen to be believed, but also have to be believed to be seen.' The diagnosis defines the treatment. And if you choose a diagnosis that makes things difficult, well, strangely enough, things become difficult. If you choose one that makes things easy, things can become easy, or easier at any rate. (We've seen *that* somewhere else before, too.)

You can imagine yourself into trouble – oh the joys of hypochondria! – and to an extent you can imagine yourself out of trouble too. The Christian Scientists would argue that you can imagine yourself out of all possible trouble (though they would call it 'faith in the healing power of God'); but it's not that simple, because you have to make sure that the imaginary world of 'I'm fit and well and whole (etcetera)' coincides with what is going on physically, in the physical world, the so-called real world. And that's easier said than done, even with something as minor as a cough or a cold.

What you can do is trick yourself into being well. Which is, in a sense, what the Christian Scientists are doing: they're passing the buck for their well-being to someone who's supposed to be Almighty and therefore capable of looking after everything that we feel we can't cope with at the moment. We do much the same kind of trickery in conventional medicine: we stick people in a hospital bed, get the nursing staff to give them some personal attention, show them some expensive-looking high-tech toys that suggest that they're probably getting better and, as long as we don't cut their insides about too much or confuse their chemistry with dubious drugs, they'll probably get well all on their own, without any specific 'thing' being done at all. To quote Lao Tsu, 'If nothing is done, nothing is left undone': although, as with 'co-incidence', it makes more sense if the hyphen is emphasised – 'if no-thing is done . . .'.

But this is also much the same as what we're doing with a pendulum: we're using a stage-prop in a complicated charade to trick ourselves into perceiving things that we couldn't otherwise see. Or tricking ourselves into a state of mind in which we no longer try, but just get on with things in an ongoing variant of beginner's luck. ('Trick' is perhaps not the best word: what I really mean here is that we need some way to prevent ourselves from getting in the way of letting the pendulum, or the healing, work.)

Another name for this is magic. Healing as magic – in any sense . . .

So anything goes. It becomes a *technology*, in exactly the same way as we've been looking at the pendulum as a technology. Using a magical approach to the technology; whatever magic happens to be.

In a technology we accept that we don't know everything: we just use what we happen to have at hand. So anything is true; nothing is true. What matters is not whether some treatment is supposedly true according to some pre-defined system – because every system and no system is true. What *does* matter is whether it's *appropriate* for that person. Efficient, reliable, elegant, appropriate.

And unfortunately for the niceties of logic, what is appropriate is almost certainly going to be different for everyone, everywhen. So true healing, true medicine is more a question of finding out what's appropriate *here*, *now*. Which is by no means as easy as looking it up in some officially-approved reference book. You have to know how to *know*; to know when the system you're used to using doesn't match up with what you've got in front of you *now*.

Thinking narrow; being wide. At the same time.

Sometimes it may well be necessary to use that too-much-preferred sledge-hammer of antibiotics or radiation treatment or whatever, side-effects and all. But sometimes it's more appropriate to indulge in sleight of hand, subterfuge or just plain straightforward trickery to prevent ourselves from getting in the way. Or just sitting and talking, spending a little time with someone – that strange form of healing called the doctor's 'bedside manner'. If it works – if you get the coincidence of getting better – we don't need to know what 'the real cause' was. And anyway, it's cheaper than drugs.

QUESTION TIME

Anyway, time to return to the pendulum. It's good at answering questions: so one practical application of the pendulum is to use it to answer questions. Using it as bait while fishing for facts.

As usual the trick is not so much the answers as the questions. Once the question is clear, the answer seems to arrive all by itself – whether you're using a pendulum or not. Developing your intuition; developing taste, judgement, wit; following hunches. Phrases like that.

The conventional idea of a technical or scientific training is actually designed to discourage you from using these aspects of yourself: hunches aren't scientific, you can't pin them down to a single cause. Which is unfortunate, because the hunches are where almost all new ideas come from, where almost all problem-solving comes from.

We're specifically trained at school and at college to be able to solve logical problems on that theme of 'Here's the question: what's the answer that fits?' But a side-effect of that is that we're also specifically trained to be unable to solve the problems that are *outside* logic, the ones that the real world and Murphy's Law really do throw at us, which as we've seen are more like 'Here's an answer: so what was the question?' It's interesting to realise that graduates going on to formal scientific research often have to be taught how to *stop* using their newly acquired analytical skills long enough to be able to observe again!

In effect, the analytical mode of thought has to be knocked out of action before you can think, or at least think of anything new. And you have to think of something new, something different, each time you get stuck, otherwise you end up going round and round in circles – ever-decreasing but perfectly logical circles.

Getting unstuck means inventing a new way of not being stuck, inventing reality.

There are many methods that are used in formal research, such as brain-storming, conceptual blockbusting and the rest. Most of them involve working in teams, which isn't all that easy if you're working on your own.

One solution is to use the pendulum, as much as a kind of ritual as for its use as an 'answering machine'. The idea, rather as we saw in the 'I've lost my keys' exercise, is to use your watching of the pendulum as a way of keeping you from thinking much about anything else – with the result that useful bits of information can arise and show themselves out of the corner of your eye, so to speak. Using the pendulum as 'thinking narrow', with your full attention on the pendulum; but sensing, listening, 'being wide', at the same time.

A nice piece of mental acrobatics. So let's try it.

SEARCHING THE LIBRARY

You need a particular piece of information. The only trouble is that you don't have a clue as to where to find it.

Search the library.

But – as is all too often the case in any form of research – you're not even sure how you'd describe that piece of information. All that you know is that you'll recognise it when you see it.

An analytical method – search every sentence of every page of every book in the hope of finding something you'll recognise – would take for ever. It's just not practical. So that's out.

You could search every likely book: but which books are likely? And even then searching every page could take a *long* time.

So it's back to inspired guesswork – which is where the pendulum comes in.

What we have to do here is trust to coincidence: to allow ourselves to squeeze in through that gap between nothing and Murphy's Law, the gap we've called Nasruddin's Law, in which useful things can happen by coincidence. Because by framing the question, the quest, the 'what I'm looking for', in your mind, you've primed yourself to recognise that coincidence when it happens, regardless of how it may be caused.

So this is using a ritual, a game, as a means both of framing the quest and of allowing the gap to happen; using the pendulum as ritual, and being open to coincidence at the same time.

Make it clear to yourself what you're looking for. Frame the question, the quest, in your mind.

As usual, don't try. It may matter that you find this piece of information: but even so, don't try, because trying harder will simply get you further and further away from finding it, until you're forced back to the brute-force-and-ignorance method of searching everything the hard way. Instead, let the information find itself, so to speak; let the information find you.

Start the pendulum moving in a Neutral mode. You want a Yes response when what you're pointing at contains the information you're looking for or something that is relevant to the information that you're looking for. (The latter is perhaps not essential, but it's what you might call a 'get-out clause' in case what you're looking for isn't in the library at all: in which case you also want to find anything that will point to it or direct you to it elsewhere or in some other way.)

Now do what you might call a sector search. Point to each section, or perhaps touch each section if having something to touch makes things more tangible; see if you get a Yes response for any of them. Note also if you get a No or Idiot response (though what those would mean depends on the context, so you'd have to sort that out yourself). Having found one Yes, do the same for each column of shelves on that section (if you had a Yes for more than one section, you'd do them in turn). Then for each shelf in the column. And then for each book on the shelf.

Don't even look at the titles of the books: let it happen by itself, don't try to analyse what's going on because the whole idea is that you're playing with coincidence, not cause-and-effect. You're conducting a sector search.

When you have a book in your hand, flip through the pages until the pendulum says 'stop' – in other words swing the pendulum in Neutral and go through the pages until you get a Yes for 'This is the page.' Or use the contents page as a list, and work through the chapters until the pendulum says Yes. Or do the same in the index. Or trust totally to coincidence, to Nasruddin's Law, and just open the book at random and see what you get.

It may look like nonsense; it probably *is* nonsense, compared to what you're supposedly looking for. But it probably does have some relevance. Look at it again: what ideas arise? What analogies does it suggest? Remember that you're dealing with the Joker's whimsical sense of humour: whatever it is, it isn't likely to be that straightforward; you'll have to think sideways a little to make sense, to put it to use.

If it still doesn't make sense, just play. Try turning the book upside down. Take the first word on the page and the last. Anything. See what ideas arise.

Follow those ideas: start the same loop again, looking for new information, searching the library, to see what new ideas arise.

It's an interesting way of doing research!

BUG-HUNTING

As I mentioned earlier, in addition to writing books, I also write computer programs for part of my living. And by far the hardest part of writing a program is not the design, or the coding, but getting the thing to work at all. Getting the bugs out; correcting all the mis-instructions that send the program blundering off anywhere but where I want it to go.

A computer program is a structure of logic: *if* this is true, *then* do that, and so forth. So in principle I ought to be able to analyse what's gone wrong with my logic. The problem is that even a small program is likely to be too big and too complex to analyse every possible condition of what might go wrong. And if the program operates in 'real-time' – in other words responds to events that happen in any combination at any time in the real world – it's often impossible to reproduce exactly the sequence of events that caused a program to crash, to go off into an endless loop of twiddling its little digits.

So in 'debugging' a program, we have to rely a surprising amount on intuition, on taste, on an awareness of what it feels like to be the program. Otherwise we'd get nowhere slowly.

The program's crashed again. You have in front of you a pile of program listings and other information that must be at least five inches thick. And – as usual – no one bothered to document their design decisions when they wrote the program: in other words, it's an almost indecipherable mess. *Somewhere* in there there's another bug. So find it. Fix it. It's your problem.

This is actually the same problem as searching the library. The brute-force-and-ignorance method – reading every single line and comparing it against every other line – will take for ever. Well, it will certainly *seem* like it, anyway. You could do it if you have to, but it's not exactly a happy prospect.

So it's back to guesswork. Inspired guesswork. Looking for a useful coincidence to help you. Which brings us back to that part of our toolkit that's 'entirely coincidence and mostly imaginary'.

Enter the pendulum again.

A ritual to encourage awareness. Thinking narrow; being wide.

A sector search. 'Where is the problem that triggered this program crash?' Point down the pile of listings, noting down (with a pencil on the edge of the stack of paper, perhaps) where you get a Yes response. You'll probably get several Yes responses: note them all down. The same with No or Idiot responses (other problems that haven't surfaced yet, perhaps?). Then look more closely at the areas that you've marked: flip through the pages until the pendulum tells you to stop. Point at each line of code on that page, and note the pendulum's response. (If you get an Idiot response, you've probably overshot in your search and are looking at the wrong page.) And see what you've got.

It probably doesn't make sense. Not yet anyway.

Look at it again. Before you discard it as irrelevant, consider what the program's doing at this stage. What's going on at this point? What values are where? What do the machine registers contain? What's in the program stack and any other side-stores? What is the state of the machine? In short, look at the program from the program's point of view at that place in the code: *be* the program at that point.

What other ideas arise as you're doing this? Thinking narrow, focused on the logic of the program; being wide, watching for ideas and possibilities and suggestions as they arise at the same time.

And round the same loop: do the scan, the sector search, through the listing again, until you find something to fix.

It does work! If you let it. But it can't work if you're trying too hard: if you're constantly talking at the program, asking it questions, you can't listen to what the program's trying to say.

This approach can apply to any 'debugging' problem. For example, as I've said before, I've watched an electronics engineer doing exactly the same with a circuit design. Feeling his way round the circuit with the tips of his fingers, sensing the component values, working out by feel and awareness the results of any change to those values. To use the old engineers' term, this is 'thinking with the hands': being aware, being wide, being open.

The point is that debugging is alogical: outside logic. It's working on logic, working on the assumptions being used in the program or whatever: and it has to be beyond those assumptions in order to look at them at all. Which leads to a tortuous way of thinking; devious, almost. Looking in that gap between nothing and Murphy's Law; looking at chance, at happenstance, at coincidence.

Putting coincidence to use.

A technology of luck, you could say. Beyond logic. Guesswork, inspired guesswork, with the pendulum as a means to improve the inspiration!

FISHING FOR FACTS

There's this new high-tech decision-making executive toy. It's called a pendulum.

Unfortunately there's no wonderful store where you can buy a magic wand to answer every question. Especially the awkward ones like 'What do I do now?' or 'How do I get this to work?' The pendulum, as you know, would only answer Yes. Helpful as ever. You're left fumbling around in the dark, trying to see when there's nothing to see. It's like driving in fog: there's something out there and I'd rather not drive into it, thank you!

What you really need is another way of thinking. And in a way the pendulum can help here, despite its penchant for unhelpful answers. So you stick a 'Gone fishing' sign on your office door, and go fishing for facts, using the pendulum on its string as bait to dangle over the muddy waters of the mind.

You'll also need a pencil and paper. And just to confuse the issue, you'll also need to use your pendulum at the same time as writing, so you may need some practice with the other hand first if your writing hand is the one you usually hold your pendulum in.

Let your mind wander a little. Take your mind for a walk, with the pendulum like a dog on a lead. It doesn't matter. Not even what you're trying to solve – it will solve itself if you let it.

You're just sitting there. Just sitting, watching the ideas drift by. The pendulum, if you like, is the float in the water, waving backwards and forwards in the currents of thought.

Just watch the pendulum out of the corner of your eye. As ideas drift by, watch its response. Write down (in a half-interested fashion) any ideas that seem interesting to the pendulum – in other words when a Yes (or even a vague Yes) response occurs. For that matter, note down in a separate column any No ideas, or even Idiot ideas. Perhaps especially the Idiot ones.

Every now and then, take a closer look at what you've written down. Point to each idea that you've scribbled on the paper: watch the pendulum's response to it more closely. Think about what those responses might mean. Only casually: don't think too hard about it. But just let it be part of the conditions – ground-bait, if you like – when you go back fishing for facts again.

And go round this loop several times. New ideas arise; the pendulum (which is you) comments on them; you write those down. You look at them in more detail; then go back to fishing again. New ideas arise . . .

Don't just grab at the first idea that comes along. There may be a better one just around the corner, watching to see what happens to this one. On the other hand, this may be the best you get, but perhaps it could be developed a little. And so on.

Fishing for new ideas; fishing for facts. Just fishing.

OUT OF TIME, OUT OF MIND?

In some ways it would be so much easier to answer 'What do I do now?' if I knew what was going to happen in the future. So perhaps if I could use the pendulum to predict . . .

Oh dear. Here comes trouble!

Yes, you *can* use the pendulum to predict the future. *If* you know what future you're looking at. *If* you know what questions you want to ask that future. *If* you know how to bring that imaginary future into the present reality now in time to be the future that you want it to be. If; if; if . . .

If you want to go completely insane playing with paradoxes, try playing with prediction. Out of time, out of mind?

But in context, working with time with your pendulum can be useful – though only as long as you realise that what you're working with is not fact, but probability: the probability that a particular coincidence will appear at a certain time as well as at a certain place.

PROBABILITY PRACTICE

What we're dealing with is probabilities: finding the most likely, most appropriate future from an infinite number of possibilities. But unlike statisticians and the rest who are busy working out the

probabilities of a particular happening according to probability theory, we're concerned with probability *practice*. Once again, putting
coincidence to *use*.

Probability theory may be able to tell us that, according to
designers' claimed statistics, there would only be a risk of a major
nuclear accident once in a thousand years or so of operation. But
this doesn't tell us *when*: it only tells us the chances. It may not
happen for a thousand years: but it could equally happen this year,
this week, this day – statistics can't tell us. And since nuclear
systems seem to have been designed primarily with the assumption
that Murphy's Law doesn't exist, the statistical guesses may not
be too good anyway.

The problem with probability theory is the same as that of geology
that we saw with water-divining: it can see some kind of overall
structure, but it can't see the detail. And it's the detail we need. We
need to know what 'then' is going to be, now. Except, courtesy of the
Joker and the paradoxes of prediction, we can't know precisely: we
can only guess. Statistically speaking, that is.

What we can also do, though, is pluck a single future out of the
morass of probabilities and see if it tastes right, using a pendulum to
say when 'then' matches the questions you're putting to it. Thinking
narrow, limiting the options around that future; being wide, to sense
whether what you see seems appropriate, seems somehow right. Not
logical at all: but *alogical*: outside logic. Practice may not always make
sense, but at least it makes more sense than theory if you're putting
that guess about the future into practice.

The more you limit the range of that future, the more likely it is
that you'll be able to get it right. 'Right' in the sense of useful, anyway.
If you try to use a pendulum to tell you what the price of gold will
be in three months' time, the best answer would be Idiot: there are
too many variables affecting it and, for that matter, too many people
pushing for it to change, which will certainly affect the way you see it.
But if you try to work out something simple, you stand a much better
chance of getting it right.

Something simple – such as the time your friends are going to
arrive at your house.

They're leaving their house this morning: as for when, you don't
know and, knowing them, they don't know either. Use your pendulum to find out.

To the pendulum, time is just another quantity. You could
point to a time on a child's toy clock; you could use a stream
of 'Will they have left by nine/ten/eleven o'clock?' questions; you

could simply count in hours and minutes until the pendulum tells you to stop.

Keep in mind the image of their leaving the house: picture them getting into their car. Visualise them; the car; the house; all together. And you want the *time* of the event of their leaving their own house: the coincidence in *time* of that event.

It will take them at least an hour to get to your house. Imagine, then, that you're inside their car with them, half an hour after leaving – whatever time that is. Where are they? Look around outside the car: what landmarks can you see? In other words work *from* a specific time rather than trying to find out what the time is. (The pendulum isn't going to be much use here, though perhaps you might like to plot on a map where they are – in other words will be – at that future time.)

And look further forward in time. You're inside the car with them at that time, even though you're also at home at this time: looking at your home from the outside as they drive up to it. What time is it now – 'now' being the time of their arrival?

You're looking for the coincidence of two times in one place: then and now, here. Working in time; through time; in imagination, by coincidence. Putting prediction to practical use.

PAST AND FUTURE

There are, of course, plenty of predictive tools in the traditional toolkit: the Tarot, the *I Ching*, runes, astrology and many, many others. All of them, you could say, entirely coincidence and mostly imaginary; but tools none the less.

The classic mistake with something like astrology is to take its predictions literally – and either believe them totally or dismiss them out of hand, according to your preference. But they look at things in a symbolic way, by analogy, by comparison, by coincidence. Without any real concept of cause-and-effect or connectivity at all: just that things happen to happen in the same way at the same time. Part of the Joker's games, perhaps.

Astrology doesn't predict events, the actual content of coincidences. It can, however, describe the context which surrounds those events, the context which gives those events their meaning. Or perhaps provide you with ambiguous-enough symbolic imagery to force *you* to look at the context around those events, which comes to much the same thing. Imagery that's vague enough, 'noisy' enough, so to speak, to allow you to resolve that paradox of 'Things not only have to be seen to be believed, but also have to be believed to be seen.'

Treat astrology as something that provides absolute facts about a certain future and you'll find yourself having some interesting if expensive discussions with the Joker. The same with the pendulum, of course: you have to interpret the results it gives you – especially the Idiot responses.

But let's assume that astrology can give us a detailed summary of *context*. A birth-chart, supposedly, can give you a detailed summary of the *context* surrounding what happens to you in life: past and future in your own life. But to build a birth-chart, you first need a birth-*time*: and that's often not available. 'Sometime in the evening' isn't accurate enough when even a few minutes can make a significant change in a chart.

So out comes the trusty pendulum. Let's say that you're doing this for someone else's birth-time rather than your own (Somehow it's easier if you don't have to look at yourself.) Out comes the child's toy clock again. 'Show me the time of this person's birth.' Build the image of that person: use a sample of them, if you have one – such as hair or fingernails – to reinforce that image. *This* person; *their* time of birth. Pointing around the clock; counting hours; Yes/No questions about time: any way you like, but just arrive at a time that's *their* birth-time. Not yours – theirs.

Getting the precise time, precisely.

Except, by another one of these peculiar twists, it sometimes doesn't seem to matter if it *is* their nominal birth-time at all. I've played this game a number of times and have on occasion been as much as twelve hours out from the officially recorded time of birth: but always somehow it's provided an *appropriate* birth-chart. You could argue if you like that that was the intended birth-time, prevented by the hospital's meddling or whatever: it doesn't matter. It's all coincidence anyway.

But that's the whole point: it *is* all coincidence anyway. A collection of images to enable you to look at things in a different way, from a different point of view. Entirely coincidence; mostly imaginary.

Tools for looking at context. Tools for you to look at your looking at the world, through coincidences in the world as you see it. Looking at past and future: and realising that they're imaginary too. The question is not so much whether it's true, but whether it's useful: efficient, reliable, elegant, appropriate.

And if it seems crazy to others: so what? That's their problem, not yours!

TWO'S COMPANY

Almost everything we've looked at so far can be done on your own. Not quite hidden in the closet, perhaps, but something like that. But there are quite a few applications of the pendulum that can only be done with two or more people.

More interesting, too.

CONFUSION TIME

It's useful to work with others for confirmation of your results, or simply to give you some encouragement. It's too easy to go off on some impossible tangent if you only work on your own.

But it's also important to realise that there are some wonderful booby-traps that can occur when you're working with others. Two's company, perhaps; but three can be a crowd.

Confusion time.

For example, there's a variant of that old trap of 'I got a response there last time, so I ought to get the same there now': and that's 'Well, *she* got a response there, so I ought to get one too.' She may be wrong, you know. You may be looking at different things. You may be defining 'here' in different ways. And so on.

In short: don't assume! Learn your *own* responses. You don't know other people. You aren't other people. You're *you*. And that means that what's true for others may well not be true for you.

The opposite applies as well: what's true for you may not be true for others at all. I remember one terrifying woman from a local dowsing society who used to run around screaming 'That's not the right way to do it: you have to do it *this* way!' It had never occurred to her that other people might be different from her, might have had different experiences from her. But everything is true, and nothing is true, all at the same time: what matters is whether it's appropriate, for you, now.

It's not easy to strike the right balance between comparing results and wandering off in a common delusion. I've fallen for that many a time: in a world where nothing is truly objective, it's a trap that's hard to avoid. The important point to bear in mind is to keep open, thinking narrow in the sense of watching the pendulum closely, but at the same time being wide, sensing for things that don't match your assumptions, watching for the Idiot response; watching for the Joker; balancing seriousness with laughter.

What we don't need either is an absence of thinking. For example, a lot of people have carried on with the research I did some years ago on 'earth energies', on so-called 'energy leys' and the like: and I must admit that I cringe when I see someone saying that their work proves that all these strange phenomena that we're recording were all laid out aeons ago by the Lemurians or the Atlanteans or some passing alien with a penchant for straight lines.

Please! Nothing's as simple as that. And it doesn't help to assign one unknown to another unknown – saying that the energies were created by some mystical super-civilisation – when both of them are entirely imaginary. Real too, perhaps, but imaginary also. To babble about Atlantis may be glamorous, but it isn't exactly useful, especially if you try to make out that it's 'absolute truth'. In Nils Bohr's words: 'Your theory may be crazy: but it's not crazy enough to be true.'

Thinking narrow, thinking clearly, precisely; but being wide, being open, being aware, to see when thinking alone is not enough.

Working together: to help each other in thinking narrow, being wide.

MESSAGE SERVICE

One game that's interesting to play as a group is what I call 'message service' – perhaps the pendulum equivalent of the telegraph. For this you need at least three people complete with pendulums, all standing astride a convenient water line.

First find your water line. A pipe would do: but we had best results – or at least more credible results – with what seemed to be natural water-flows underground. Lines that we 'saw' with the pendulum that gave a Yes response on the pendulum to 'Is this water?', and yet wasn't a pipe – in other words what a water-diviner would be looking for. (If this isn't obvious here, you'll see what I mean soon enough when you put it into practice.)

Park two of your group on the line that you've found, but out of sight of each other so that they can't guess what the other is doing. If you have more than three, park them on the line as well: but you need one person spare as an observer-cum-recorder. Everyone's pendulum is swinging gently backwards and forwards, or whatever Neutral happens to be.

Now each of the group on the line gyrates their pendulum in turn: either Yes or No. Push the pendulum into the movement you want: don't bother with niceties like asking the thing to do it for you. The others on the line should get the same movement: with practice, without trying. Perhaps. Sometimes they'll get their own response for Yes, though, if it was a Yes that's coming down the line and their Yes response is different from the sender's. Just see what happens.

Don't try: just do it.

There's nothing to prove: let it happen. The key point is laughter: tell each other that perhaps the last thing you want is for anyone to think 'hippopotamus' . . .!

Let everyone have a turn at being sender and receiver.

Now change the rules. Instead of winding up the pendulum yourself, ask it to do a Yes or whatever. Don't tell the others what you're sending – Yes or No – but perhaps it may be easier for all concerned to say *when* you're sending. Cut down on interference and all that.

Change the rules further. Don't even bother to let the pendulum go into a Yes or No mode: just think it, imagine it, and send that image down the line.

And change the rules still further. Draw a line on the ground. An imaginary line. Send your imaginary Yes and No down the imaginary line.

Perhaps even dispense with the line. Send your Yes and No direct. Build an image of that person that you're sending it to; build an image of what you are sending; you're sending it *now*, and receiving the image back in return. However, it's all coincidence, and entirely imaginary.

Yet it works. Or at least something does, because you're getting the coincidence of what she's sending, of what he's receiving, and so on. A stream of Yes and No responses, most of them the same as what we imagined was sent. Except nothing was sent: it was all imaginary. Along an imaginary water-line; and then just on a totally imaginary line.

It's not so much a question of whether it's true, as whether it could be useful. And obviously it could indeed be useful in some circumstances. An imaginary message service. Making use of coincidence. But the trick is going to be finding ways to make it efficient, reliable, elegant, appropriate – *that* problem again!

WORDS AND IMAGES

Obviously this game has a fancier name: it's a crude example of what most people would call 'telepathy'. But we don't need fancy labels: we're simply concerned with whether what we're doing has any *use*. A technology of mind; a technology of luck; a technology of coincidence. A technology of you using yourself to the fullest extent, without worrying too much about whether someone else says it's impossible.

All we have is information, and its interpretation. The information can come from anywhere – but it's up to you how you use it. Or, for that matter, how you see it.

So go back through all that stuff that doesn't fit the conventional assumptions about the world. And see if you can use it. It doesn't matter if it's true: is it any use? If not, just file it away somewhere: you never know when it might be useful.

A good example is dreams: a morass of words and images and symbols and anything else, all thrown together into a tangled heap. Some of it is what we would call 'garbage collection' in the computer trade: recent information such as today's discussion with a friend and a television programme from last night jumbled together during the process of being sorted into neat piles for storing away in the mind. Other bits come from further away: fragments associated with some memory that came up while talking to someone else three days ago. Yet other pieces are merged with sensings while you were asleep: a gust of wind rattling the window-pane mixed up with yesterday's complaints from the cat. And yet others might well come from what is supposedly 'outside' yourself: such as someone else reading this book and trying to make sense of a connection between marmalade for breakfast last Tuesday and that it's raining in Guatemala at the moment.

A jumble of information, all of it true, none of it true; jumbles; juxtapositions. Correlations; connections; coincidences.

Ignore it all, and you get nothing. Try too hard, interpreting every tiny symbol in every dream as some warning from on high – as I've seen so many people do – and what you'll get is Murphy's Law; what you'll get is the Joker playing games at your expense. But somewhere in the middle is the *use* of this mess: somewhere in the middle is Nasruddin's Law, in which things happen crazily, miraculously, irregularly, irreverently. If you can see them. If you can let yourself see them.

You can use the pendulum to help in this. Over a period of time, get into the habit of noting down your dreams: you'll need to keep a notepad and pen beside the bed, because the images disappear from the mind almost as quickly as they come. Train yourself to wake up and record them; or spend a little time in the half-awake state in the morning reconstructing them in your mind before you get up out of bed.

After that, what you'll now have is a written list of images that arose in the night. Now go through this list with the pendulum, asking a question such as 'Is this significant?' for each. Note the pendulum's responses down beside each image: Yes, No, Idiot or whatever. And follow this up as we did when we talked about 'fishing for facts' earlier: see what other images arise as you go down the list with the pendulum, and make a note of these too.

And this is where all that stuff about 'thinking narrow, being wide' comes in. Taking information as information, not unchangeable fact; but at the same time being open to finding the *context* that gives that information its meaning.

So this really *is* entirely coincidence and mostly imaginary. Content + context = meaning. Sometimes, anyway.

By now you should be getting better at finding that meaning – with practice!

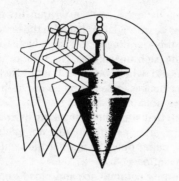

7 · WHERE DO WE GO FROM HERE?

We've looked at some techniques and some applications. Some of them will be immediately useful to you; others won't. Not yet, at any rate. We've even looked at a little theory, if only to recognise that theory isn't always all that helpful.

Fine. So where do we go from here?

The first step, perhaps, is to go through it all again. Especially if you started at the back of the book. The use of the pendulum only makes sense when you use it. In *practice*.

In other words you have to *do* it as well as read about it. Then it will make sense – perhaps.

And then, more to the point, it becomes a useful tool. Part of the toolkit. Though *not* the only tool in the toolkit: not the 'big hammer' of thinking. And a tool to be used, not a tool to be used *by*. That *would* be crazy.

With that done, now is the time to look elsewhere. All those books on dowsing, both with the pendulum and with other instruments

112

such as the L-rods and the forked stick: more tools, more techniques, which you can use. None of them the answer, the way to do it: all of them new (or at least different) ways of tackling a problem. All of them true, none of them true – for any problem.

Remember always that we have a set of guidelines: our dowsing must be efficient, reliable, elegant, appropriate.

The other 'elsewhere' to look is other people. Dowsing societies, special interest groups, research projects, or just the local health-food co-operative. 'There's safety in numbers, you see,' as the old song goes: if other people are crazy enough to be using the pendulum, then perhaps you aren't so crazy after all. And you can learn from others; practice your techniques; simply get some encouragement in what you're doing with the pendulum. You're always on your own, of course; but you're on your own with support from others. It helps.

What you do with it, though, is up to you. It's your pendulum; your world. And your responsibility, too.

INVENTING REALITY

We've come a long way. As promised, we've talked about toolkits, about markers and pointers, about positive and negative, about coincidence and things imaginary, and practical matters such as drainpipes. And also about skills, about intuition and judgement, and ways of thinking backwards, sideways, upside-down: a maze of paradoxes and mental acrobatics.

All these things we can put to use.

We still don't know how the pendulum works: you can choose your own explanation and it will still work – if you let it.

What matters is not how it works, but how it's used.

Efficient, reliable, elegant, appropriate. And that's up to you – how you use you.

Inventing reality; inventing your own reality.

And all done with a piece of string, a weight of some kind, and a little thought – or lack of it.

THE IMAGINARY PENDULUM

But since we've made most of the toolkit disappear into imaginary worlds, we may as well do the same with the piece of string and the weight, and leave ourselves with an imaginary pendulum.

There are good reasons for this. Perhaps the best one is what I call 'Not in public, please.' We're still in an age in which people get upset at seeing things they don't understand, or which don't fit their tidy definitions of what is 'proper' and what is not. And they can get quite upset at seeing you use a pendulum in a church or in the street, for example. If what you're doing doesn't fit their world, it's frightening for them: and that fear is not something to encourage. Quite the opposite, in fact.

There's also this simple point called embarrassment. Using a pendulum seems to be something that people prefer to do behind closed doors, in private. It's not considered nice to be crazy. And wandering up and down the street waving a ring on a string is a quick way of being seen as crazy – that's what it feels like at times, anyway.

And there's also a matter of practicality. If you can carry an imaginary pendulum around with you, you don't have to worry about losing it, or leaving it in your other coat, or having it punch holes in your jacket pocket. It's always there. Entirely imaginary, of course, but it's always there.

Imagine it now: the pendulum's swinging gently back and forth on its thread, in the Neutral mode. Except it isn't there.

But it doesn't have to be: you can imagine it to be there. Sure, it takes a little more awareness, a little more skill in holding that imaginary world in mind, but that's something you're learning.

Tell the imaginary pendulum to give a Yes response. You can see it: even if no one else can, because it isn't there.

You can imagine it. And if you can imagine it, you can use it.

Entirely coincidence; and now almost entirely imaginary. Being put to practical use.

The only trouble is: people would think you were even crazier if they thought that you were using an *imaginary* pendulum. It's bad enough with a real one ... So don't bother to tell them: just do it!

So now imagine being without the pendulum at all, and getting the same results in answer to questions you frame to yourself, the same clarity of Yes and No. And Idiot. Feel it in your fingertips; feel it; sense it in any way you can.

In the end, the best pendulum, which is also the most invisible pendulum, is no pendulum at all. Instead, you use yourself.

Learning to walk without the crutches; learning how to be aware, how to *know*.

Inventing reality, indeed.

A DOWSER'S TALE

Perhaps a story of my own can illustrate this.

I've long been fascinated by the pendulum and its uses. Ever since I was a child in fact. But I'm no master dowser, and I probably never will be: I haven't the patience, the obsessive commitment that I'd need for true mastery of the skill.

I suppose you could suggest that I'm one of those people of whom it's unkindly said: 'Those who can, do; those who can't, teach!' But that's a little unfair, because my interest has always been much more with studying the learning process: how people learn skills, learn judgement, learn awareness.

Learning how to learn.

The pendulum is my test-case, my experimental platform. Traditionally it's assumed to be a 'gift' which few people have: yet we can see now that it's better described as a skill that anyone can learn. And learn the basics in a matter of minutes, enough to put it to practical use.

In reality, it doesn't actually matter at the end of this as to whether I can use the pendulum or not: in fact the whole thing could be a trick if you want to think of it that way – although a trick to trick you into working with other aspects of you that are also you. What does matter is not whether I can now use the pendulum for what you want to do, but whether you can. And that, after all, is the whole point of the book.

For ten years, though, I was using a pendulum intensively in research work of my own, on the ancient standing stones and stone circles of Britain. A study of what we called 'earth energies', since that's what we seemed to be finding. And it was that study that showed me not only the usefulness of the pendulum, but also, in the end, its uselessness on its own, without a wider awareness to put it into context.

It all began with a college trip to visit two Welshmen, Bill Lewis and John Williams – an engineer and a lawyer – to talk with them about their experiences and their understandings of the old stones.

They showed us how to sense energies in bands around the stones: energies sensed not just in the movements of the pendulum, but in my fingertips, tingling, like static electricity, like a mild electric shock. Sometimes strong enough to push me over, push me to the side, away from the stone. The traditions of 'dancing stones' suddenly became a tangible reality. I could quite literally feel the stones dancing in my hands. Welsh standing stones, the ruins of a past

The Rollrights

time, with names ringing like chimes: Llanfihangel, Maenclochog, Gors Fawr, Bryn Celli Ddu.

Enthusiasm can be infectious. It was for me – totally.

So I spent weeks living in a van beside a stone circle called Rollright, in central England, its stones aptly described as 'gnarled and rotten like an old man's teeth'. Assisted by occasional visits from friends. Recording changes in 'polarities' with the pendulum; noting down the pulsing, the changes, the breathing of the site, as the cars hurtled by on the road outside the circle.

Knowing that we were looking at something that was happening not in the past, but *now*.

What is this energy? How does it change? How does it work? What correlates with what? And what were the stones built for anyway? Trying to understand what appeared to be going on; seeing that the patterns I saw were becoming more and more complex the more I studied them, yet failing to understand why.

Teaching others to dowse, to use the pendulum and the other tools; to teach others how to see and sense these elusive 'earth energies'.

Then years of study; more teaching; watching the stones and the patterns, expecting them to answer my questions. And more questions. And at so many different sites, ancient and modern, so many more patterns of energies, both below ground and above. Finding that we could measure the energies, or some of their side-effects, with needles and dials and meters: ultrasonics, infra-red, microwave, micromagnetics and many others. Energies imaginary *and* physical, at the same time. The Dragon of folklore coming alive, coming to light. More and more complex; trying to find the pattern behind the patterns.

Mapping, plotting, co-ordinating; teaching, writing, talking; thinking, more thinking. Being scientific, we thought; a new objective science.

More findings: the energies have definite effects on people, on plants, on animals. Trying to find ways to manipulate the energies, as a new technology, to change them and their effects. And wondering, long and hard, as to whether we should; as to whether we had that right.

And still trying to find out what the patterns really *are*.

Looking in ever finer and finer detail, at something that is forever elusive; something that refuses to stay still long enough for us to catch. Like a dim star at night, it simply vanishes if you look straight at it: but yet somehow it's still always there.

Until finally, for me, a day trying to map energy lines below Glastonbury Tor, with its enigmatic tower dominating the Somerset

117

landscape. A hundred lines, it seemed, all changing, all with varying senses and properties, across a stretch of road no more than a hundred yards long. It didn't make sense.

Then suddenly a sense of laughter from nowhere: the Joker . . .

It wouldn't make sense, because it couldn't – not looking that way. I'd been looking too closely to see anything at all.

What I was seeing was what I expected to see. 'Things have not only to be seen to be believed, but also have to be believed to be seen.' Seeing the place through a filter of preconceptions and assumptions: so that what I saw depended as much on my assumptions as on what was 'really' there. Real and imaginary: at the same time.

So at last accepting the end of the pretence of 'being objective': because what I was seeing about the place was as much about myself in the context of the place. I was both the observer and the observed, with the place as a mirror: an interaction between myself and the very real energies of the place. And what I was seeing was me.

It was like looking closer and closer at a sweater: I could see patterns, and then patterns within the patterns, and then patterns within the patterns within the patterns. But I'd forgotten to look at the same time at who was wearing the sweater, let alone why.

Looking so hard, I'd failed to see at all. Trying so hard, my thinking ever narrower, being so serious about it all, I'd left no room for laughter. In asking and asking the same questions, again and again, I'd forgotten to listen. And the old stones had much to say: about time, about context, about simply being.

Awareness. Thinking narrow; being wide. Listening.

So now, if I visit a stone circle or a standing stone, a holy well or a grove of trees whispering to the wind, I leave my dowser's toolkit behind. Instead, I listen; and sometimes, just sometimes, I can hear the laughter of the stones as they move through the steps of their courtly dance.

The pendulum has its uses. But in the wrong place it's the wrong tool: it can be worse than useless. A tool for seeing, that ends up preventing us from seeing.

In the end, the pendulum doesn't matter at all. Not in the slightest. But the awareness you learn in learning to use it does matter. Totally.

In fact in some ways that's all there is.

You using you. You knowing you.

Enjoy yourself!

APPENDIX:

CONTACTS

You can only learn so much from books and from working on your own: eventually you really do need others against whom to test your ideas and experiments, and from whom you can learn more.

Any good bookshop could no doubt advise you of likely contacts in your area, or of suitable events to go and see – or more to the point, to join in. But perhaps the most important place to make contact with is one of the national dowsers' societies: from them you're likely to learn most of all.

The *British Society of Dowsers* is the oldest, founded in 1933. It started out as something of a military club, but those days are now long since gone: most members are now actively involved in some aspect of dowsing rather than trying to find out 'how it *really* works'. Perhaps the most common interest is in health and healing, although every other aspect, from civil engineering to archaeology and beyond, is represented. The society holds an annual conference and several lecture meetings each year (usually in London); there are also many local groups scattered throughout the country which run their own lecture schedule and, in some cases, training courses. Contact the Secretary, Michael Rust, at Sycamore Cottage, Tamley Lane, Hastingleigh, Ashford, Kent TN25 5HW; telephone Elmsted (023 375) 253.

The *American Society of Dowsers* is a large, active body with many local 'chapters' scattered throughout the United States. The Society's base is in Danville, Vermont; the annual convention there, in September, takes over all the facilities of the town for workshops and seminars for the several hundred attendees. (Perhaps there's some truth in the rumour that when that many dowsers come together looking for water, they tend to find it one way or another, because it almost always rains then!) There are probably more water-dowsers in the American Society than the British, perhaps because of a greater national need for water; but again almost every aspect of dowsing is represented. In addition to the national convention, many of the local chapters or groups of chapters put on their own conventions: Denver, for example, or the West Coast convention in Santa Cruz in July each year. To contact them, you'd probably best contact the national centre first, at Dowsers' Hall, Danville, Vermont 05828–0024; telephone (802) 684–3417.

INDEX